Child sexual abuse

providing for victims
coping with offenders

Proceedings of two conferences held on

2nd February 1998
and
12th March 1998

together with additional papers

Edited by
Stephanie Hayman

The Institute for the Study and Treatment of Delinquency

CHILD SEXUAL ABUSE
providing for victims
coping with offenders

Published 1998 by
The Institute for the Study and Treatment of Delinquency
King's College London, Strand, London WC2R 2LS

Tel: 0171 873 2822   Fax: 0171 873 2823
E-mail: istd.enq@kcl.ac.ul
Web site: http://www.kcl.ac.uk/orgs/istd

Cover photo taken by Jessica Hayman

ISBN: 0 901541 54 0

Typeset, designed & produced by Amberwood Graphics

CONTENTS

Page

Foreword and acknowledgements   4

Part I

People Like Us: The Review of Safeguards for Children Living away from Home   8
Sir William Utting

Investigating the exploitation of children   17
Nick Davies, Journalist

Female sexual abuse of children; 'the ultimate taboo'   25
Dr. Michele Elliott, Director, Kidscape

Child prostitution; whose failure?   34
Allan Levy, QC

Children's advocacy centres; an American model of response to
inquiries into child sexual abuse   39
Sophie Hughes, Planning and Review Manager, Hereford Social Services

Bearing the unbearable - working with child abuse   42
Dr. Roger Kennedy, Consultant Psychotherapist, The Cassel Hospital

Part 11

Practical difficulties encountered by police, probation and social services;
the key issues for inter-agency working within the *Sex Offender Act 1997*   46
Alan Bowman, Director of Social Services, Brighton and Hove Council;
Penny Buller, Chief Probation Officer, East Sussex;
Mike Lewis, Sussex Police; **George Smith,** Sussex Police

Assessing risk and dangerousness; problems for the police in operating
the register   58
Ray Wyre, Independent Consultant

The difficulties encountered when investigating abuse that has taken
place in the past   64
Terry Oates, Detective Inspector, Cheshire Constabulary

Some thoughts arising from the recent conference   81
Tony Butler QPM, Chief Constable, Gloucestershire Constabulary

Never mind the facts, where's the story?   84
Gill Mackenzie, Chief Probation Officer, Gloucestershire Probation Service

The Dutch perspective   87
John Staps, Head of Youth and the Vice Squad, Rotterdam

Speakers Details   94

FOREWORD and ACKNOWLEDGEMENTS

ISTD held its first conference on child sexual abuse in November, 1996. As the consequent Report *Child Sexual Abuse: Myth and Reality* mentioned, two major inquiries were underway at the time and it was intended that ISTD would return to the subject once there was more in the public domain to be discussed. Sir William Utting's report *People Like Us: The Review of Safeguards for Children Living away from Home* provided the impetus for the conference *Child Sexual Abuse; Is Anyone Listening?*, held on the 2nd February, 1998 at King's College London and we were delighted to be able to welcome Sir William himself to speak about what he and his team discovered during their long months of deliberation. This conference focused almost entirely on the needs of child victims of abuse.

Just before it took place we were approached by Sussex Police about the possibility of holding a further conference, one which looked particularly at the difficulties confronting various agencies as they attempted to cope with sex offenders residing in the community. We had already scheduled a discussion of the practical issues surrounding the implementation of the register of sex offenders, as required by the *Sex Offenders Act 1997*, for the February conference but, from the furore surrounding the case of Robert Oliver, it was clear that the subject needed to be dealt with in greater depth than was possible then. Consequently, the conference *Practical issues when dealing with sex offenders in the community* was held on the 12th March 1998 at the Law Society. Even the briefest of looks at the following days papers showed that the subject was a matter of wide public concern, irrespective of how responsibly individual papers chose to treat the conference itself. There are some who feel that such matters should be discussed away from the public gaze - and certainly not within sight of assembled television cameras - because the questions raised are of great sensitivity, with the debate needing to be freely conducted by those who have immediately to deal with the problem. However, it could equally be said that this reluctance to have an open debate adds to the concern felt by the general public who, without evidence to the contrary, feel their concerns about safety are ignored; the debate need not be about specific individuals or details, but should nevertheless be taking place.

We have decided to combine the papers from both conferences in the one report because the issues dealt with are inter-related. *Part One* begins with **Sir William Utting** and his discussion of *People Like Us: The Review of Safeguards for Children Living Away from Home*. He covers the main recommendations of the report and comments 'it was not clear to the Review Team that parents of children living away from home are necessarily aware of the risks to their children's welfare'. He argues that children need a consistent legal framework to protect

4

them from assault and abuse and concludes with a call for a unified government response to the issues discussed in the report. **Nick Davies** spoke in gripping detail about what he discovered when researching for his book *Dark Heart* and this paper is an edited transcription of what he said. He talks about the difficulties encountered by anyone attempting to expose the activities of paedophiles and of the culture of secrecy which has inhibited and pervaded the many inquiries into abuse. **Michele Elliott** writes of the growing recognition that women are also abusers. Until fairly recently it had been assumed that abuse was an overwhelmingly male offence and it is only now that 'survivors' of such abuse have started to tell their often harrowing stories of damaged lives. **Allan Levy** discusses the question of child prostitution, particularly the fact that 'the criminal law... is generally being used against children instead of being used against those who abuse them'. These plenary presentations were followed by workshops and two of these are included in this report. **Sophie Hughes** writes about child advocacy centres. Crucial to their success is an 'holistic approach to the children ... and the same team of workers (being available to the child) throughout the process of inquiry'. **Roger Kennedy** writes of the particular combination of nursing and therapy that is unique to the Cassel Hospital, where whole families may be admitted for intensive, residential rehabilitation which can be spread over many months.

Part Two begins with a joint paper by **Alan Bowman, Penny Buller, Mike Lewis** and **George Smith**, all of whom were closely involved in dealing with the problems created by the arrival in Brighton of the convicted paedophile Robert Oliver. Together, they outline an inter-agency response to the difficulties they faced and end by asking 'at what stage does a local operational difficulty become a national issue, requiring central support and direction?' **Ray Wyre** also spoke at the first conference and was asked to enlarge upon what he first said at this event. In looking at the use of registers for sex offenders he comments that all too often such registers and protocols are not delivering an adequate service; he thinks it is all too easy to hide behind registers and not to confront the need to manage the majority of sex offenders who will inevitably be released into the community. Many of the cases involving paedophiles that have reached court cover abuse that has taken place over a number of years and has involved many victims. **Terry Oates**' paper discusses the difficulties facing police forces investigating abuse that has allegedly taken place in the past and how staff may best be assisted in bringing together all the relevant available information necessary for a prosecution. He also emphasises the great need to support victims through what may be a lengthy and painful procedure.

This report also contains two short articles that were not heard at the conference. Both Tony Butler and Gill Mackenzie were invited to comment on the issues raised from their particular perspectives as lead speakers on sex offenders for, respectively, the Association of Chief Police Officers and the Association of Chief Officers of Probation. **Tony Butler** discusses the power of the media in his article and reflects that, while sensational newspaper headlines sell newspapers, they tend to achieve nothing else. He also updates the situation by outlining initiatives taken by the Home Office since March, particularly the formation of a national steering group to look at the issue of high profile sex offenders. **Gill Mackenzie** also comments on the role of the media and highlights how irresponsible reporting may lead to vigilante action against people totally unconnected with the case. She gives a brief review of recommendation contained in HM Inspectorate of Probation's report *Exercising Constant Vigilance: The Role of the Probation Service in Protecting the Public from Sex Offenders*. Our report concludes with a paper presented by **John Staps**, who looks at the way sex offenders are handled in Holland. Part of his message is one repeated by other contributors to this report; that children are not generally at risk from the unknown, dangerous stranger, but are infinitely more likely to be harmed by those known to them, such as a family member.

Neither of these conferences would have been the success they were without the help of many people. Our speakers, as always, contributed in a most generous manner and provided us all with a great deal to ponder and debate. The February conference was in some ways a reprise of the very first one because we were again fortunate to have both Jon Snow and Dr. Barbara Kahan sharing the duties of chair. To both we extend our thanks. The second conference was feasible because of the very active collaboration of Sussex Police. Their financial assistance made possible a subsidised registration fee and probably contributed to the largest attendance we have ever had for one of our conferences. Paul Whitehouse, Chief Constable of Sussex, kindly agreed to chair the proceedings and we are most grateful to him for that. Mention must also be made of the considerable help given by Colin Knight, of Sussex Police, who so effectively ensured that the various agencies were fully represented at the conference.

Stephanie Hayman
May 1998

PART ONE

PEOPLE LIKE US
The Review of Safeguards for Children Living away from Home

Sir William Utting

Introduction

It is a particular pleasure to speak at this conference because members of the team who worked with me on the Review were able to attend your earlier conference in November 1996. The report *Child Sexual Abuse: Myth and Reality,* which published papers from the conference, was a great help in orientating us on the subject at a critical point in our work and I am grateful to the distinguished contributors to that conference.

I intend:
- to start with the dangers to children living away from home;
- to say something briefly about the principal settings in which children live away from home children's homes, foster care, schools, and the penal and health services;
- and to end with some general comments about staff, parents, children, government, personal information and criminal justice.

The Review was instituted by the Government in 1996 as part of its response to the disclosure of past abuse in children's homes. The terms of reference included children living away from home in England and Wales, with particular reference to children's homes, foster care and boarding education. Its purpose was to find out whether the extra safeguards introduced by *The Children Act 1989* and by later action were strong enough to prevent further abuse. Four colleagues worked with me on the Review: Cathy Baines, John Rowlands, Marian Stuart and Roz Vialva. Roger Kent undertook a parallel exercise in Scotland, and his report was published at the same time as ours.

The remit of the Review extended well beyond sexual abuse to all kinds of harm that might be inflicted on children, but it is sexual abuse that grabs public, political and professional attention. It seemed important to the Review to keep these concerns in the context of the totality of abuse and other harm inflicted on children. Our experience was of a distinctive strain of sexual abuse merging into a much broader band which contained elements of physical, sexual and emotional abuse. Further along the spectrum of harm is the concept of systems abuse, which became a vivid reality for us as we exhumed the activities of incompetent institutions and indifferent authorities.

Dangers

We needed to form a view of the principal dangers that children living away from home should be protected against, and constructed, methodically if not scientifically, a typology of three groups. People who are sexually fixated on children are attracted to careers and voluntary work which affords easy access to them. Paedophiles may be talented, socially acceptable and successful in the worldly sense. They may also be sexual terrorists who inflict dreadful and probably permanent harm on the children they seduce, brazen when challenged, unscrupulous, incapable of shame. Estimates of their numbers working in services for children away from home varied widely. Safeguards are needed which prevent their employment in the first place, detect the conduct of those who evade initial scrutiny, and ensure effective disciplinary and criminal proceedings against them.

The second and, in my view, much larger group consists of adults and children who may harm children physically, sexually and emotionally. The pressure cooker atmosphere of residential life releases inclination towards the sadistic use of power, provides opportunities for aggressive and abusive behaviour that are not encountered in the community, subjects individuals to abnormal stress or unfamiliar temptation, or corrupts them by bad example. These may be opportunistic rather than consistent abusers, but some of them persist in such varieties of abuse that they are no less chilling and dangerous than paedophiles.

The third group includes elements of individual misconduct and incompetence, but they are subsumed within the predominant characteristic, which is that of the failing organization. Human error at many or all levels produces an institution which fails to implement its own policies, in which incompetence and indifference lead to damage on a large scale. Ethical conduct seems an essential ingredient of competent performance in the world of human services; weak and unethical organizations allow individual misconduct to flourish. They also inflict damage on a wider scale by failing to promote the welfare, development and future prospects of the children they are responsible for. More children are likely to suffer a different, generalized harm through these failures than are harmed by positive acts of abuse. Issues bearing on overall effectiveness are inseparable from questions of safety. The less effective institution is also likely to be less safe. Quality protects.

We assumed that, in general, children living away from home were more vulnerable than children living with their parents to abuse by other people. Submissions to the Review identified certain children as particularly vulnerable: young children, children looked after by local authorities, disabled children, children with emotional and behavioural difficulties, and children with parents overseas. Particular care is needed in promoting and safeguarding their welfare. The needs of disabled children, for example, require an integrated approach by

9

education, health and social services authorities. Children who appear in more than one category accumulate additional vulnerability. Children looked after by local authorities acquire significant stigma.

The Review is clear that additional safeguards are needed for the majority of children living away from home. Children continue to be harmed in all settings. The report makes more than 150 fundamental or detailed proposals for making them safer.

Children's homes

We concluded, however, that abuse on the former scale is now unlikely in children's homes. Far fewer children live in them; 8,000 in England and Wales in 1995 compared with 40,000 in 1975. Homes are much smaller, with an average capacity of ten children. Procedures for recruiting staff have improved greatly as a result of Norman Warner's report *Choosing with Care*. Managers are more alert to the problem of abuse, but there are no grounds for complacency. The Review supports Burgner's proposals (in *The Regulation and Inspection of Social Services, 1996)* for registering small children's homes. We also support his recommendations for powers of emergency closure, notices to remedy deficiencies in registered children's homes and an accelerated appeals process. Moreover, residential care is not consistently effective in helping residents grow into mature and independent adults. Government action is urgently needed to drive up the standards of residential care by implementing a national strategy.

Foster care

Two thirds of the children looked after by local authorities in England and Wales now live in foster homes. The decline in residential care has contributed to major changes in the nature of fostering. The whole of its population is more vulnerable than it was. Many children entering foster care have already been abused, or have disturbed behaviour. Carers face more complex and stressful tasks.

The Review Team was disturbed that inspections of foster care disclosed, among much good practice, some worrying disregard of basic safeguards. Local authorities must follow existing regulations and guidance. The Review also recommends a government code of practice to cover the recruitment, selection, training and support of foster carers. Private foster carers and independent fostering agencies should be registered by the local authority.

Boarding schools

There are about 110,000 children in boarding schools and residential education in England and Wales, ranging from the most privileged to the most disadvantaged children in society. There are 80,000 in independent boarding schools registered by the Registrar of Independent Schools. Most of the remaining 30,000 are children with special educational needs. About half are in schools provided by local authorities, the rest in schools approved by the Secretary of State or registered as children's homes.

Section 87 of *The Children Act 1989* required independent boarding schools to safeguard and promote the welfare of pupils, and opened their arrangements for doing so to inspection. This is generally working well, although arrangements for bringing deficient schools up to a satisfactory standard need urgent overhaul. The Review recommends that the provisions of Section 87 are extended to the remaining residential schools, many of which are run by local authorities and accommodate numbers of particularly vulnerable children.

In addition, education and social services authorities should unify systems for placing, financing, reviewing and supporting emotionally and behaviourally disturbed children in boarding schools. They should be assessed by social services authorities as 'children in need' under *The Children Act 1989,* and appropriate services offered to them and their families.

In the case of independent schools, the Registrar should be empowered to deal speedily with serious concerns about the welfare of pupils. Swift and coordinated action is needed to deal with serious situations revealed by inspections and child protection investigations. At present the Registrar is compelled to travel procedurally by the equivalent of a slow boat to China. When, after official letters and inspectorial visits, he is at last able to issue a Notice of Complaint, this still allows at least six months for improvement to be made. That may be reasonable for putting right an educational problem, but is far too long to wait if an institutional crisis is harming children's welfare. The cumbersome machinery is no match for quick-witted and unscrupulous proprietors.

There is also a strong public interest argument for extending the Secretary of State's powers of inquiry into children's services, under Section 81 of *The Children Act 1989,* to include all boarding schools. Policy makers, professionals and parents would benefit from the information made available about the activities of abusers and the effectiveness of preventive and remedial measures.

Penal and health services

Last year the number of children under 18 in prison service establishments rose to 2,600. Prison is not a safe environment. The Review was particularly concerned by the prevalence of bullying, ranging from physical brutality to verbal intimidation, in spite of Prison Service strategies for countering it. The prevalence of sexual abuse should be investigated. We urge that the principles of *The Children Act 1989* be incorporated into the rules governing children in prison service establishments. The Government should end remands to prison for boys under 18 forthwith. I urge you to read HM Chief Inspector of Prison's Thematic Report on Young Offenders, a magisterial and comprehensive survey, which was published on the same day as the report of our Review.

About 15,000 children in England and Wales spent periods of more than a month as in-patients in 1994/5. The majority were receiving treatment or surgery for medical conditions. Some were disabled and others had psychiatric conditions. Issues relating to safety and welfare arise as keenly in hospital as in other settings. The general safeguards recommended by the Review apply to health settings as elsewhere.

General issues
The principles for recruiting and selecting staff in *Choosing with Care* (the Warner Report) have been implemented by most local authorities. The Review believes that they should be applied in all settings in which children live away from home. Conformity should be a condition of registration, approval, accreditation and the award of contracts.

The report does not proceed to discuss whether action should be taken to review all the people (other than foster carers) currently engaged in work with children away from home. Such a project might be desirable in theory but we are far from being able to realize it. Major difficulties exist over the accuracy of predictive tests, the basis for dislodging staff because of what they might do, the logistics of the exercise and its effects upon the morale and performance of major services. The problems of extending sensible recruitment practices across the whole sector seem to the Review quite enough to attempt in the immediate future. If that basic work is universally achieved, it provides a platform of knowledge and experience from which to attempt work with the whole staff. In the meantime, managers worried about individuals are able to make use of the developing tests and consultancies in this field.

The wisdom and feasibility of defining parental rights and responsibilities in statute are matters that extend far beyond the terms of reference of the Review. *The Children (Scotland) Act 1995,* however, says that parents have both a responsibility and a right 'if the child is not living with the parent, to maintain personal relations and direct contact with the child on a regular basis'. It seems almost inevitable that similar expectations should be held of parents elsewhere in the United Kingdom. Moreover, it was not clear to the Review Team that parents of children living away from home are necessarily aware of the risks to their children's welfare, that they are informed about all the safeguards which should be in place, or even that they are enabled to play a full parent's part in ensuring the safety of their children. A general statement of their responsibilities would surely be helpful.

In addition, all organisations which care for children living away from home should provide parents with full information about their arrangements for keeping children safe. This might include information about recruitment procedures for staff, codes of conduct, anti-bullying policies, child protection procedures, discipline and control of children, complaints procedures, access to telephone, and arrangements for health and pastoral care. Parents should always know the identity and location of registering and inspecting authorities. The Review also recommends that the Government sponsors a programme on public health lines to increase the understanding of parents and relevant staff about the risks to children's welfare and the means of reducing them.

We believe that a consistent legal framework is needed to protect all children living away from home against assault, abuse and ill-treatment. Children's rights to physical and personal integrity should be protected in all settings, and should not permit any kind of physical or psychological violence. Higher levels of protection or security are needed in some places, but they should wherever possible derive from the needs of the child rather than the characteristics of the setting. In addition, specific policies are needed to combat bullying and both racial and sexual harassment.

A right of particular importance to the safety of children is their right to speak for themselves. Comments suggested, however, that young people were often unable to share in decisions being made about them in spite of the provision for this in The Children Act. In particular, participating in case reviews was often ineffective in their eyes since they were poorly prepared and inadequately supported for a process that was unfamiliar and some found intimidating. Formal complaints procedures were not much used by children for similar reasons; the Review believes that children who wish to complain should have the support of an independent advocate. Children eligible for the services of an Independent Visitor could not depend on receiving them because such schemes were not generally available. The Review believes that the concept of independent visiting should be broadened and applied to all looked after children who are willing and might benefit from it. The Review warmly welcomed the development of children's rights services and argues that they too should be offered to all looked after children.

The young people we consulted were among the most emphatic in stressing the importance of a controlled and structured environment in keeping them safe. They expected the adults who care for them to face up to their responsibilities for securing and maintaining order. Comments from care staff were dominated by anxieties about physical restraint and about physical assault on them or other children. The Review believes that these should be met by combining further central advice with clear managerial expectations and support, and training staff in nonviolent methods of control as well as physical restraint where that is likely to be required.

Services for children are now dispersed among a larger number of providing agencies. A greater responsibility rests on the centre to secure consistent standards nationally in protecting and promoting the welfare of children. We were worried, however, by the volume and complexity of the regulations and guidance that affected children living away from home. Much of this is valuable and valued, but needs simplifying and reordering if practitioners are to apply it consistently.

This task requires both care and time; the Review accepts that it should be undertaken 'in the medium term', but regards this as one of the Review's most important recommendations. Piling guidance upon regulation may satisfy bureaucratic and political needs, but it obscures the clear view of priorities which is indispensable to managers and practitioners. The Department for Education and Employment and the Department of Health/Welsh Office should dovetail their revision of arrangements for regulating homes, schools and private fostering in order to clarify responsibilities and remove overlaps and gaps. These are exploited by dubious providers to avoid complying with the intentions of legislation and to prolong processes of complaint and investigation.

Enforcement of regulations is critical to children's safety. Regulation which is not monitored or enforced is positively harmful, creating a sense of confidence for which there is no foundation. Inspection - national and local - is an indispensable element in monitoring and an important factor protecting children away from home. It is not, however, a substitute for the routine monitoring managers should undertake. Its primary function is to serve the public interest providing an additional safeguard for vulnerable people.

Monitoring must be backed by a vigilant registering authority which possesses the power to act quickly and forcefully when need arises. The Review endorses the value of constructive relationships between the registering authority and the bodies it supervises, exemplified by a positive approach to overcoming the problems which agencies providing services for children typically encounter. There is a need, however, to speed up the process of applying sanctions when situations endangering children are revealed. This requires greater determination by registering authorities to act decisively in the interests of children. They also need some additional powers.

Communicating information about people unfitted to work with children is complicated legally and procedurally. Information is held by different agencies and according to different criteria. Criminal records, the Department for Education and Employment's List 99, and the Department of Health's Consultancy Index are well used and valuable. Their effectiveness would be improved by better co-ordination, faster procedures, and wider and more consistent use by parts of the constituency. The central difficulty, however, is the level of corroboration required for personal information which is to be stored and may be transmitted to a prospective employer. The Review is aware of the harm that innocent people suffer if inaccurate or unfounded information about them is passed on. Its impression overall, however, is that current restraints inhibit the passage and recording of information about people who are dangers to children. The Government should extend the legal protection of employers in such cases, and the proposed Criminal Records Agency should access other approved lists as part of its own checks.

I did not expect when I began work on the Review that it would lead me to the criminal justice system. The way in which this deals with people accused of offences against children, particularly sexual offences, became important to the Review for three reasons. Firstly, children living away from home are, other things being equal, more vulnerable to abuse. Secondly, transmitting information about potential employees who are dangers to children depends heavily, and at present disproportionately, on criminal records; the system cannot work effectively if guilty people are not being convicted. Lastly, the lengthy and detailed processes of investigation generated by the requirements of criminal justice are experienced as oppressive by children, parents, staff and institutions. The processes themselves become obstacles to the disclosure of evil and the subsequent protection of other children against its perpetrators.

Criminal justice lags behind other social institutions in responding to the volume of information about sexual abuse which has become available in the last 20 years. Children appear to be more at risk than adults. Conviction rates have declined to an alarmingly low level. Young children and disabled children are peculiarly vulnerable because of the reluctance to regard them as competent witnesses. Patent abusers of children are not convicted or even brought to trial. The Review believes that justice would be assisted by the implementation of the remaining recommendations of the Pigot Report. The principal need, however, is a wide ranging review of the arrangements for prosecuting alleged sex offenders against children.

A unified Government response is required to the issues discussed: in particular, reinforcing children's rights, defining parental responsibility, revising and enforcing regulations, transmitting personal information and reviewing the prosecution of sexual offences against children. The Secretary of State for Health leads a Ministerial Task Force in preparing and implementing the Government's response to the report.

People Like Us is published by The Stationery Office at £25. A free summary is available from Department of Health, PO Box 410, Wetherby LS23 7NL

INVESTIGATING THE EXPLOITATION OF CHILDREN

Nick Davies, Journalist

I know it is conventional for a speaker to spend ten or so minutes telling you what he or she knows and then to answer questions, but I would like to reverse that by taking 15 minutes to tell you the things that I do not know and then ask you the questions. I have a selfish reason for doing that, as I am in the middle of investigating this subject for The Guardian; child abuse, paedophile rings, the way the system reacts to these. I find it extremely difficult and I need some help, so that is the selfish reason. But there is also a deeper reason which is that, in so far as I am working on this particular subject I am powerfully struck by how difficult it is to get reliable information about it.

I did not set out to look at children being abused; I kept stumbling into it. For example, about four years ago Warwick Spinks was arrested in Hastings and he was put on trial in Lewes, accused of raping two homeless boys whom he had found in the streets of London. He was also accused of abducting one of them and selling him to a brothel in Amsterdam. That was an unusual story, so I set out to look at it and soon discovered that those charges were part of wider allegations against Spinks and his friends in Amsterdam. They had allegedly been making 'snuff' movies and sexually abusing children, to the point of death, in front of a video camera for future distribution and sale. That allegation came about because a number of informants, quite independently of each other, had spoken to the police about these events and some had mentioned Spinks in relation to them. The police had put an undercover officer in close to Spinks and, unaware that he was being taped, Spinks had boasted at great length about his involvement. I investigated this and turned it into an article for The Guardian and a rather weak television programme, the weakness being that despite all the statements and the accumulating evidence about these films, at the end of the day, we could not find the tapes, nor could we find anybody reliable who had seen them. Consequently, if you were to ask me have there been 'snuff' movies made by child pornographers, in this country or Amsterdam, the answer would be that I do not know. You can ask police who specialise in this area and they will tell you the same thing; they have often heard of them, but have never found them. So this is a very specific area of ignorance.

I stumbled into the subject again, when I started researching for my book *Dark Heart*, which is about poverty in Britain. Over and over again, without my looking for it, I kept coming across abuse of one sort or another. An important experience was about four years ago when I came across two young boys selling themselves in a fairground in Nottingham and it made me realise my own naivety. I had not known, until I met those boys, how simple a fact of life it has become in almost every city in this country that someone can buy a child and have sex with him or her. Not just somebody who is technically under the age of consent, but somebody who is male or female, aged 11, 12 or 13; those who are clearly children. I was trying to find out why there were quite so many children involved in this and the thing that became apparent at the outset was the really alarming fact that it is not just the many pimps who were trying to exploit them by pushing them out onto the street. The most terrifying thing about the children I talked to in numerous cities around the country was their gross willingness to sell themselves. I am not trying to embark on some paedophile fantasy; this is about the emotional damage which has been experienced by some children. Talking to them, there were two things that the vast majority had in common. One was that they were, or had been, residents of children's homes and the other, which ultimately I felt was more important, was that in equally high proportions they had grown up on impoverished estates. Their lives had collapsed around them and their individual families had collapsed. The community had also collapsed: employment had been sucked out of it; links between neighbours and friends had disintegrated; there were drugs; there was violence; there was drink. By the time they were ten or twelve years old they thought prostitution was an appropriate, almost attractive, way to lead their lives. But there are still lots of questions unanswered. In almost every city in this country you can find these children selling themselves, but how many there are I do not know. Does anybody know? Do the police know? They do not. All the police do is collect figures for convictions of children, which is grotesque in itself. The idea of punishing these children is wrong-headed in the extreme but these are the only figures the police have. This does not tell you the reality of what is going on in the streets; this simply tells you of the occasions when the police have had a crackdown, and arrested some children. If the police have their right identities and ages, these children are then filtered into the statistics.

As I went further and further into investigating poverty, more examples of abuse came out. I spent two days with different social workers in different places, talking to them about the scale of child abuse; sexual, physical and emotional. Talking to them, two points emerged. One was that, particularly on very poor estates, the scale of abuse was staggering. I drove around an estate with one particular social worker and he pointed out various houses where abuse occurred as we went by. The proportion of that poor, disintegrated populace who had fallen into abuse was just staggering. The second thing that emerged from these two social workers was that they were deeply uncomfortable about saying this, because they felt it was a libel on the poor and on the communities and families they were working with. Because of that reticence there is another black hole; no-one admits how bad it has become. The point I want to make is that the blurring of the picture is not acceptable. It might be thought a dangerous thing to say that poor people are more likely to abuse their children than the wealthy - even though the wealthy may do it, too but if that is the truth it is crucial to speak out, in order to remove that other black hole.

There are deeper reasons for our ignorance. One is that child sexual abuse is one of the least reported crimes. Over the last ten or fifteen years we have become familiar with the fact that adult victims of rape have not reported the offence and there have been changes in procedure to encourage reporting. Whatever applied to adults, in their desire to conceal their victimisation, clearly applied even more to children. I may be telling you things that you know already, but I have talked to a lot of children in the last few months who have been abused as well as those who are adult survivors. Amongst them all there is always deep confusion about their plight, with comments such as *'oh, I thought it was happening to everybody, when everybody got home from school they got raped by their father, I just thought it was normal There was the fear of breaking up the family if I said that my stepfather was doing things. Then everything would fall apart. We would have no money and, my mother would be furious.'* There are additional factors. As well as being the least reported crime it is also possibly the least believed of crimes. If a bank manager should go to a police station and report that his bank has been robbed, he generally has no problem in persuading the police that the crime took place. Crimes against property are inherently like that, whereas the crime of child sexual abuse is the opposite. Any trial will probably involve no outside witnesses and the one key witness will be a child. Accusations by children tend to be treated with undue scepticism and, when a trial does take place, the child will then be cross-examined by adults in an aggressive, professional way in an effort to undermine the child's credibility. Unlike other sexual offences, this abuse is deliberately concealed by its perpetrators. There is evidence of organization by paedophiles, as is revealed in details emerging about children's homes in North Wales, and you rarely get this with sexual offences against adults. As Sir William Utting said, institutions which are involved or affected by child abuse conceal this, either deliberately or through incompetence. Taking North Wales again as an example, the survivors of abuse - an expression I am not terribly happy with - who have been giving evidence to that inquiry have identified 148 adults who abused them during their time in those children's homes. It may well be that some of those allegations are mistaken, or even false, but on the whole they are credible because they overlap so frequently with each other, the same people are constantly referred to. During the 20 year period in which those attacks are alleged to have happened there were 27 police inquiries, none of which even began to identify the scale of abuse. Even if all those allegations were false the police inquiries should still have acknowledged that the allegations had been

19

made and then gone on to decide whether they were true, but they did not. Similarly, during that period there were 13 inquiries by social services and again none of these came anywhere close to identifying the scale of the problem in their subsequent reports. So my ignorance is not just a matter of professional incompetence, but the result of a deeper secrecy. One of the main points I wish to make is this; secrecy matters hugely. Our ignorance matters because there is a subsequent lack of political pressure as a consequence of our absence of knowledge. If we knew the whole truth how much political pressure would be generated, how many changes would need to be made? The core point is that the child protection system we have at the moment - for all the good work that has been put into it, all the thought and all the research - does not protect children. It does not do its job and our ignorance is the key fact which allows that to remain the case. When I talk about child sexual abuse being the least recorded crime, this ignorance has a specific relevance.

One of the most appalling things is the lack of pro-active police work in this area. This is not a criticism of the individual officers who work on child abuse. Every force in this country now has a child protection unit and those units do good work, as anybody who has had any contact with them would agree, but the units are reactive. When cases come up through the social services or elsewhere, there are these specialists who can handle them. To a limited extent they may be able to investigate, although what tends to happen is that if they become involved in an interesting case the ordinary CID will come thumping in and take the case over. How many forces in the country have a pro-active unit which is going out to try and detect unreported child abuse? The Metropolitan Police has 16 officers in the paedophilia unit. I think the West Midlands may have converted its old obscene publications squad into a similar sort of unit. In Cheshire, where they have had massive problems in their children's homes, there is now a unit that has emerged from that investigation and I think that is working proactively, but that is about the sum of it. You compare that with what happens with the investigation of robbery, burglary or drugs. In London alone there are hundreds of officers working in these fields, yet there are just 16 who are working to investigate paedophiles. There is a deep structural reason for this happening because over the last 18 years every branch of the public service has been encouraged to develop performance indicators by which they can measure their work. These indicators tend to be quantitative and, for the police, this means they are being told by the Home Office to clear up reported crime. The end result is that there is no encouragement to dig up unreported crime. Some brave chief constables have started doing this and the Metropolitan Police deserve full credit for setting up a paedophile unit which goes out and uncovers unreported crime. Yet the Home Office is saying to chief constables 'frankly, if you want your power, prestige, promotion and your budget, do not dig up unreported crime.' That may sound cynical, but the people saying that to me most often are the chief constables themselves, when explaining why they have not got paedophilia units. The result is that we have the crime of child sexual abuse being committed, almost certainly on a very large scale, with a high proportion of it being unreported and almost no attempt being made to detect it.

Yet despite those difficulties some cases do come up through the criminal justice system, leading eventually to a conflict of interest between the social services and the Crown Prosecution Service (CPS). I cannot see how you reconcile them. The social services and the police officers who work in this field will say that the Memorandum of Good Practice requires that the paedophile is charged, yet the Memorandum suggests that if you are interviewing a child who is alleged to be the victim of abuse, you may interview them only once, for an hour and no more. There is some room for discretion, but that is the general thrust of interviewing within the Memorandum. The social services will tell you this is crazy; you have a child who is frightened and confused, yet interviewers are given an hour to come up with everything. Furthermore, they have to do this, within the constraints of not asking the child a direct question. They may not say 'were you and your step-father intimate?' They cannot ask 'did he touch you?' Instead, they must say 'where were you last night and what happened?' A confession may not be encouraged at all, so there are real problems in getting disclosure. On the other hand, a decision is made to prosecute and officials say 'look, we have people who are accused of serious offences and they may be innocent; they have a right to have evidence gathered in a way that is safe and proper and if we allow people to go on for hours at children, asking leading questions, there is a risk that we will get false evidence'.

There is a further point, which is whether or not a child who has been a victim of abuse can have therapy in the period of time between the offence being discovered and the trial. It is clear that the CPS is worried by therapy taking place in case it is seen as rehearsing the witness, or because of the chance that the child might come up with allegations which had not been made during the brief one hour interview. While the CPS cannot forbid therapy, it discourages it quite frequently. Yet from the point of view of social services, whose primary concern is the care of the child, it is desperately important to start looking after the child, who cannot wait for up to twelve months for help. This needs to be reviewed because, of those cases that are coming in to the CPS, an alarmingly high proportion are not actually being taken to court and, of those cases that do get to court, an alarming high proportion collapse. What does that suggest to the social workers and police officers who are dealing with cases on the ground? It begins to suggest 'don't take these cases to court', so if there is a child who is a victim of alleged abuse, there is no point to subjecting that child to a medical examination because the

CPS will not proceed. The result is that we end up with even less evidence. The hole gets darker and darker, we know less and less and the system is freezing up. There has been recent research suggesting that resources should best be placed in prevention rather than the investigation of child abuse. This is a fantastically dangerous thing to say because, in that context, the social services management are encouraged to say 'why bother at all?'.

There have been prevalence studies which suggest between 30-60% of the population have been victims of some kind of sexual abuse. I find that hard to believe, but the fact that something is hard to believe does not mean it is untrue. So what is the truth? I have the impression that there is an increase in the amount of abuse. Am I right to link that to the growth in poverty - or is there some other reason? Has it always been like this? There is something quite profound in psychosocial terms that happens when adults sexually abuse their children.

There is also a particular question about ritual abuse. I feel very uncomfortable with the official consensus that seems to have developed which says that this is all false and a fantasy inspired by religious fundamentalists. It seems to me unsafe to adopt that position, yet in practice that seems to be the way in which the Home Office has moved.

I will end with one final thing, which is an example of the system not working. Warwick Spinks, whom I was talking about earlier, was arrested, convicted and received five years for abducting and raping children. He was in a probation house in South London last autumn, when the new Sex Offender Act had been introduced, and he was approached by a probation officer to register his details so that they could be passed to the police. Spinks simply walked out and he sent a postcard to the probation office, postmarked Gatwick, with a picture of Amsterdam on it, saying 'see you soon'. Since then, for reasons I cannot unfortunately divulge, I know that he has been to South Africa, Frankfurt, Prague and Moscow. Heaven knows what he is doing, but he is a really dangerous man and the fact that he can simply walk out and travel the world simply goes to underline the key point, which is that the child protection system does not protect children.

Nick Davies then answered several questions about the role of the media in reporting child sexual abuse. The following is an amalgam of what he said.

Question: We, as professionals, are often tied down because we cannot give information about a person on trial before the day of conviction. That immediately means that the source of information used by the media when preparing an article in advance, is not necessarily going to be the source with correct information. How do we deal with the media in terms of their polarising the debate? Have you any suggestions for us, as to how we as practitioners can deal with all of this?

Nick Davies: On your first point, the problem you are dealing with is contempt of court. If somebody has been charged and is awaiting trial then the story is sub judice and you are not allowed to do anything that would create a serious risk of substantial prejudice to the trial. The key point you have missed is that this does not include talking. In the run up to the trial you can talk to me privately as much as you like about the person concerned, without any fear, as long as I am not in the jury, nor a witness. I, however, may not publish this information before the conclusion of the trial. As long as you have a trusting relationship with the journalist you are dealing with, that should not be an obstacle. I commonly work on researching background to be published the day after the trial finishes. I am dealing with all sorts of people and that kind of misapprehension is common but unnecessary.

The second point was about newspapers with a pre-disposition not to be interested in the truth. Newspapers are completely immoral; they do not really care and they do not stick to their principles in any respect at all. What they want are stories - and to sell newspapers. If you are in a position to help a journalist you can trust with information I would urge you to do so.

Child sexual abuse is a terribly difficult area to report for other reasons as well. One is that as the law appears to stand at the moment we cannot identify juvenile victims, or any victims of sexual offences. For example, in Holland I saw a video of ghastly abuse by a man and a woman against two young boys. It was quite clear from the language used on the video and also from some of the background details that this was filmed in England; an English married couple, using their children for profit. It was also clear that this has been happening over a period of time as the video showed twelve different scenes and you could see that the boy was growing up. I know of police in this country who have got an earlier video showing the same family, with one of the two boys being horribly abused. It is really ghastly stuff, yet neither they nor I appear legally able to take the photographs of these boys, or indeed their parents, to publish them and say 'who are they? Will somebody show us where they live so that everybody can get in there and rescue these children?'. I have got The Guardian lawyers working on trying to find some loophole in the law so that we can publish the picture of the paedophiles; we want their faces in the paper so that people can identify them. However, there is an ethical issue. On the one hand it is bad for a child to be publicly identified as the victim of abuse, with the consequent stigma and possible ostracising. On the other hand, the evidence on the tape is that the abuse has been continuing over a period of time and therefore the primary concern is to get to that child and break up the situation. We need to put the parents into the criminal justice system and do whatever can be done to care for the children.

The other difficulty is the law of libel. It is such an inhibition to our ability to investigate seriously, particularly if you are looking at people who have trade unions or professional bodies willing to back them in legal action. By way of example, I know of a particular priest who sixteen years ago was suspected of abusing choir boys in his parish. There was an internal inquiry by the church, as a result of which they moved him to another church and, years later, similar allegations surfaced. He is crying out to be identified, yet I must put together the two problems; my not being allowed to identify his victims and whether he will sue if I get it wrong, or even if I get it right.

FEMALE SEXUAL ABUSE OF CHILDREN; 'THE ULTIMATE TABOO'

Dr. Michele Elliott, Director, Kidscape

My mother sexually abused me

Mother tried to own me, making me solely her possession. She kept me so isolated from other people that I never had any friends or confidants. Partly it was her way of keeping our 'secrets' safe, and partly it was her way of making sure that I loved only her. She was so jealous of my relationships with other people. She said that she had me so she'd have someone to love her. Nothing was ever mentioned about my being loved.

I was so brain-washed into feeling sorry for her that I could not have blamed her for the sexual abuse, even if I had wanted to. Using sympathy and guilt worked wonders for Mother, enabling her to manipulate me into just about anything. She told lies upon lies to make me feel sympathy for her. She's still doing it. What hurts the most about being sexually abused by your mother is the total isolation. If Mother could not love or nurture me, why did she have to keep me so isolated that I could not get love from someone else? It made me grow up believing no one loved or cared about me. I still find it difficult to believe. I don't think that all the love in this world and the next will ever be enough to fill the void of not having known love, caring or nurturing all those years. I feel so bad inside that I cannot fathom anyone even wanting to love me.

I am anxious, depressed, tearful, unable to eat, unable to sleep and unable to function. Mostly I stay in bed covered with several blankets, staring into space. I feel I'm nothing special. It's like I am nothing. I expect nothing, I ask for nothing. I merely accept what life dishes out - good or bad.

The woman who wrote this had been sexually abused by her mother from the time she was a baby until she was 16 years old. She is now 40, the mother of a seriously disturbed ten-year-old daughter and married to a man who was himself sexually and physically abused as a child. She has been bulimic, suicidal, agoraphobic and self-mutilating. Yet, she only recently was able to tell and be believed about the sexual abuse and has now started therapy. When she was 30 and about to give birth she told a doctor about the abuse and her fears. He told her

...not to be so silly - mothers don't abuse children sexually. Maybe you are worried about being a mother, but don't let your imagination run away with you.

25

Only men abuse

Of course, ten years ago doctors and other professionals were only just finding out about sexual abuse of girls by men, so it is not surprising that the doctor would have been sceptical about a woman saying she had been abused by her mother. Indeed, I remember being presented with my first case of sexual abuse in 1968 and being totally unprepared for such a revelation. I did not believe it possible that an eleven year old had been sexually abused by her stepfather, a bank manager.

Over the years, we have all learned that child sexual abuse is a much greater problem than anyone had imagined. Brownmiller[1] , Rush[2] , Miller[3] , Bass[4] , Butler[5] , Herman[6] , Sgroi[7] and countless others wrote about the problem and women started coming forward to talk about the abuse they had suffered at the hands of men. The statistics indicated that the overwhelming majority of victims of sexual abuse were girls sexually abused by their fathers.

We accepted that because we could only go on what people told us. The books and articles concentrated on female victims, and male abusers. Then adult men started talking about the abuse they had suffered as children - again from men. Statistics projected a boy to girl ratio of victims variously as I : 6, 1: 9 and 1: 12. This was disputed by Porter, Colao and Mitnick who, on the basis of their work, concluded that the ratio of girl to boy victims was much closer. They indicated that perhaps 40-50% of victims of sexual abuse were boys[8] . It seemed that boys were equally at risk from sexual abuse by men. Indeed, in a survey carried out by Mrazek et al in the UK it was found that 98% of the reported abusers were male[9].

Women could not do such things

Although society has begun to recognise that men abuse children, the possibility that sexual abuse of children could be perpetrated by women causes enormous controversy and distress. It is thought that even raising the possibility of women abusing detracts from the much larger and more pervasive problem of male abuse of children. However, the fact that there are women who sexually abuse children should not be used to diminish the scale of the problem of men who sexually abuse children. What it does mean is that perhaps the accepted knowledge about child sexual abuse needs to be re-examined.

I remember vividly giving a talk at an RAF base several years ago and stating that abusers were men. At the end of the talk an officer came up and, with tears in his eyes, said 'it isn't only men, you know - my mother did it to me'. He walked away quickly before I could respond. It made me think that maybe we should *at least* give the victims of female sexual abuse permission to talk.

26

Victims begin to tell

Then on a local radio phone-in programme we raised the issue of child sexual abuse by women. The presenter and I talked for a few minutes before the calls started coming through:

Finally someone is willing to open up the subject of female sex abusers and really listen to us. This is fabulous - a day I thought I would never see. I am a 58 year old man who was sexually abused from the age of four to twelve by my aunt ...

A woman said:

My mind knows it wasn't my fault - that it was her dirt, her filth, but it's also mine: I grew with it as part of my body, dressed with it, ate with it, cried with it, slept with it. I can't seem to separate myself from her. Yet I felt and feel utterly, utterly alone and evil to the core. Knowing how she used me hurts beyond all physical pain. It means the end of the hope that I was really loved by my mother.

A man in his fifties disagreed that it was abuse:

Looking back it seemed no great drama. Even though I was only seven years old I knew how to fondle her and suck her breasts. Oral sex lead to full intercourse which my mother and I engaged in until I left home, aged 23 ...

We had more calls than we could deal with and by the time I got back to the Kidscape office, it was apparent that this was an issue which would not go away. The letters started arriving the next day:

During the war, my brother and I were evacuated to a house in the country. The woman who took care of us made us touch her. She had friends over and we had to engage in all kinds of kinky sex. We were terrified...

Rubbish - women don't sexually abuse children. It must have been the children misunderstanding motherly love ...

My teenage babysitter began sexually abusing me when I was six. It went on for about four years. I actually thought that babysitters did that to all the kids until we got another babysitter. When I tried to get her to have oral sex, she told my mother and I got into trouble. Believe me, I kept it all a secret until now. It was bad enough being abused though some of it I liked. What was worse than the abuse was being in trouble for something I didn't even understand and certainly could not control. To this day I hate all forms of physical contact and the thought of sex makes me physically ill.

The letters and calls went on and on - from men and women who were sexually abused by their mothers, relatives, babysitters and other carers. Most had never told or had not been believed. Many had been unable to find anyone willing to talk or listen

Professional denial

One 60-year-old man said:

I tried to tell my therapist when I was 35. She told me that I was having fantasies about my mother and that I needed more therapy to deal with it. In reality, my mother had physically and sexually abused me for as long as I could remember. The abuse was horrific, including beatings and sadomasochistic sex. It took a lot of courage for me to tell. When she (the therapist) didn't respond, I quit therapy and spent the next 15 years in hell. I began to think that maybe I had just imagined it all, but why were the memories so vivid and in such detail? Just hearing that this has happened to others has helped to restore my sanity. Maybe now I can find someone who will listen and believe me. Sixty years is a long time to wait.

Sixty-five per cent of the survivors who tried to tell a therapist, doctor, teacher or other professional were not believed the first time they disclosed. Overall, 86% of those who tried to tell anyone were not believed the first time they disclosed.

Why has it taken so long?

Why has it taken so long to bring out the problem of female sexual abuse? Female sexual abuse seems to be more of a taboo because:

* Female sexual abuse is more threatening; it undermines feelings about how women should relate to children.
* It has taken years for people to recognise that children are sexually abused, but that sexual abuse has been placed in the context of male power and aggression. Women are not supposed to be sexually aggressive and the male power theory eliminates them as possible abusers, unless they are coerced by males.
* People find it difficult to understand exactly how a woman could sexually abuse a child. They are not seen to be capable of this kind of abuse.
* When adult survivors of female abuse have told their stories, they have often met with the rebuttal that they are fantasising. A child recently told that her mother had sexually abused her, along with the child's father. The therapeutic team took the view that she was clearly projecting and fantasising. The abuse by the father was never in doubt. Only after a second assessment by a well-known team at a children's hospital, was the child believed.
* Current statistics indicate that sexual abuse of children by females is rare. Estimates are that 5% of abuse of girls and 20% of abuse of boys is perpetrated by women[10]. Previous statistics indicated that child sexual abuse was rare,

even by males. That has since been shown to be untrue. Statistics are based upon what we are told and may give a false picture if some victims are not telling.

Not telling
The issue of victims not telling was highlighted after the Kidscape First National Conference on Female Sexual Abuse in March 1992. The television programme *This Morning* opened up a hotline for callers to talk about abuse by women. In the course of one day, they had over 1000 telephone calls. Ninety per cent of the callers had never told anyone about their abuse before that programme. The vast majority of the callers were women.

It is possible that bringing the problem of female sexual abuse of children into open discussion will unleash a flood of stories and change our perception of the role of women in child sexual abuse. It is equally possible that we may confirm that abuse by women is rare.

What do we know?
How many of the victims of female sexual abuse are boys? How many are girls? Of the 398 cases discussed (in *The Ultimate Taboo*) approximately 27% were men and 73% were women.

Do victims of female abuse suffer in similar ways to victims of male abuse? Like the victims of male abuse, their lives have been dramatically affected. They have: turned to drugs, alcohol, solvents, often attempted suicide and may have gender identity problems. One man, made to dress in girl's underwear by his abusers, has continued this behaviour into adult life and has difficulty with relationships. A disturbing aspect of some of the cases is the hatred of, and violence towards, women and girls that some of the men admit feeling. The abused also often have:

• difficulties maintaining relationships
• self-mutilated
• been anorexic or bulimic
• suffered chronic depression
• suffered from panic attacks
• become agoraphobic
• in some cases, sexually abused children
• been fearful of touching their own children

How much has abuse by mothers affected the adult survivors? Those who were sexually abused by their mothers seem to have an overpowering need to find bonding mother-love. Many of the survivors say that, though they hate their mothers for what they did, they still want to be loved by their mothers and would not confront them, as one woman said 'with flowers, let alone with the abuse that she perpetrated on me'.

Was the abuse always negative?
Six per cent of the male victims said that the sexual relationships with their mothers and other female members of the family, had been wholly beneficial and natural. Some of these relationships continued into adult life.

One difficulty for male victims is that the idea of the older women 'initiating the boy' into the joys of sex, is often the subject of jokes or is viewed with approval. One Canadian man related how a female relative had:
acted out her anxiety on me when I was twelve. I was supposed to like it, but I have found women repulsive over since.

This myth of the boy enjoying sex with older women is just as harmful as the myth that girls 'ask for sex from older males'.

One per cent of the women in this study-felt that the abuse was in some way beneficial. Some have said that the abuse sometimes felt good, which caused them considerable pain and confusion.

Are women forced to abuse by men?
It is often assumed that, if a female has sexually abused a child, it must have been done either with a male partner or under the influence of a male partner. Yet, more than three-quarters of the women and men say they were abused by female abusers who acted alone and often there was no man in the family at that time. However, the number of cases is small - 398 people. It would be wrong to generalise without proper representative research.

Who are the abusers?
The women who were abused reported that the vast majority of their abusers were related to them. When abuse was perpetrated by two abusers in the family, the mother was almost always involved (in 100% of dual female abusers and 95% of dual male/female abusers, the mother was one of the abusers). The co-perpetrator in these cases was the grandmother, aunt, father, stepfather or brother. When a single perpetrator was reported: 70% were mothers; 7% were grandmothers; 7% were stepmothers; 13% were babysitters; and the remaining 11% were aunts, sisters, teachers and nuns.

The male victims reported that 94% of their abusers were related to them. When a single perpetrator was reported 73% were mothers and 5% were stepmothers.

When two perpetrators were reported, mothers were abusers in 45% of the cases, along with sisters, grandfathers and other males; 22% of dual abusers were stepmothers; and 33% were babysitters and family friends.

Cycle of abuse
The abused who admitted sexually abusing children were a minority in the study. Six per cent of the female victims said they had abused children; 23% of the male victims reported abusing children. It is quite possible that others had abused, but did not feel comfortable about disclosing the abuse.

Types of abuse reported
The kinds of abuse reported by the survivors included: touching genitals; oral sex; penetration with objects; sucking breasts; forced mutual masturbation; intercourse; and a combination of beating and sexual abuse.

Age of child when abuse began
Seventy-five per cent of the victims in this study were able to determine how old they were when the abuse started. Eighty-three per cent of the women who could remember said the sexual abuse started before the age of ten; 16% were between the ages of five and ten; 1% were between the ages of ten and fifteen. Fifty-five per cent of the men reported the abuse started before the age of five; 35% were between the ages of five and ten; 10% were between the ages of ten and fifteen.

Conclusion
The survivors are beginning to provide us with some sketchy details. Ninety-six per cent of the men and women said the abuse they suffered dramatically and adversely affected their lives. That is not surprising. Seventy-eight per cent of the survivors said they could find no one willing to help or believe. That is profoundly disturbing. Some said they were told that the abuser must have been male and were offered help to remember the 'real' abuser.

Uncovering cases of female sexual abuse has been traumatic. There is a strongly held view that the issue of female sexual abuse should not be raised publicly, but should be dealt with in private. A journalist in a recent article in a national newspaper insisted that it was wrong to give all this attention to female sexual abuse. All this attention? There has been little attention paid to female sexual abuse. There are few books and articles to help us understand how to deal with even the small number of cases of female abuse so far reported. Evert wrote the first survivor account[11]. Welldon devotes considerable space to the issue of female incest[12] and Mathews et al have published the first study of female abusers[13]. Allen published a comparative analysis of female and male child abusers[14]. The literature review by Jennings in *Female Sexual Abuse: The Ultimate Taboo[15]* confirms the paucity of materials available.

There is still concern that any attention paid to female sexual abuse will detract from the major problem of abuse by males. There is no question that abuse by males is still statistically the largest reported problem. What is disturbing is the idea that suppressing discussion and acknowledgement of female sexual abuse has prevented people disclosing for fear of going against established opinion.

Perhaps we will eventually confirm the statistics that 95% of sexual abusers of children are men or perhaps we will have to re-evaluate the whole issue of sexual abuse. If the response to *Female Sexual Abuse of Children.- The Last Taboo* is any indication of the problem, then we will have to re-evaluate. In a period of only four months, there have been hundreds of letters and telephone calls from adult survivors. It is frightening to think that there may be thousands more who are waiting for the right question or the right time to tell. More worrying are those who do not tell, but who take out their pain on themselves and their families. The implications for health care professionals are enormous.

Acknowledgement: This article is based upon a chapter in *Female Sexual Abuse of Children: The Ultimate Taboo* Harlow: Longman 1993

References
1   Brownmiller S. *Against Our Will* Harmondsworth: Penguin Books, 1975
2   Rush F *The Best Kept Secret.- Sexual Abuse of Children.* New York: McGraw-Hill, 1980
3   Miller A. *Thou Shalt Not Be Aware. Society's Betrayal of the Child.* London: Pluto, 1985
4   Bass E, Thorton L (eds). *I Never Told Anyone: Writings by Women Survivors of Child Sexual Abuse.* New York: Harper, Colophon Books, 1983
·   Butler S. *Conspiracy of silence: The Trauma of Incest.* San Francisco: Bantam Books, 1979
6   Herman J L. *Father-Daughter Incest.* Boston: Harvard University Press, 1981
7   Sgroi S. *Handbook of Clinical Intervention in Child Sexual Abuse.* Lexington Books, 1982
8   Knopp F H. 'Introduction'. in. Porter E. *Treating the Young Male Victim of Sexual Assault* Orwell, Vermont: Safer Society Press, 1986
9   Mrazek P M, Lynch M. Bentovim A. Recognition of child sexual abuse in the United Kingdom, in. Mrazek P M. Kempe C H. *Sexually Abused Children and their Families.* Oxford: Pergamon Press, 1981:35-49

10 Finkelhor D, Russell D. Women as perpetrators. In: Finkelhor D. *Child Sexual Abuse, New Theory & Research.* New York: Free Press 1984:171-85

11 Evert K, Bijkerk L When *You're Ready: A Woman's Healing from Childhood Physical and Sexual Abuse by Her Mother* Rockville, Maryland: Launch Press, 1987

12 Welldon E. *Mother, Madonna, Whore.- The Idealisation and Denigration of Motherhood* New York: The Guilford Press

13 Mathews R, Matthews J K, Speltz K. *Female Sexual Offenders. An Exploratory Study.* Orwell, Vermont: The Safer Society Press, 1989

14 Allen C. *Women and Men Who Sexually Abuse Children: A Comparative Analysis.* Orwell, Vermont: The Safer Society Press, 1991

15 *Jennings K. Female child molestation. a review of the literature. In: Elliott M, ed. Female Sexual Abuse of Children: The Ultimate* Taboo. Harlow: Longman 1993:241-25 7

CHILD PROSTITUTION; WHOSE FAILURE?

Allan Levy Q.C.

Child prostitution has been variously defined. It has been said to be 'the provision of sexual services in exchange for some form of payment, such as money, drink, drugs, other consumer goods or even a bed and a roof over ones head for a night'. 'Child' refers to a person under eighteen. In a recent United Nations (UN) document emanating from the Centre for Human Rights in Geneva, child prostitution was described as 'tantamount to exploitation and victimisation of the child precisely because it undermines the child's development. It is detrimental to the child both physically and emotionally and it violates the child's rights.'

I think that many people would say that child prostitution does unequivocally involve exploitation. The 1996 UN document, *Sexual Exploitation of Children*, covers child pornography aswell as child prostitution, and includes a definition of the sexual exploitation of children as 'the use of children (under 18 years of age) for the sexual satisfaction of adults. The basis of the exploitation is the unequal power and economic relations between the child and the adult. The child is exploited for his or her youth and sexuality. Frequently, although not always, this exploitation is organised by a third party for profit.' The Council of Europe defines child sexual exploitation as 'the sexual use for economic purposes of a child or a young person, which violates, directly or indirectly, human dignity and sexual freedom and endangers his or her psycho - sexual development.'

Globalization
In recent decades the phenomenon of the sexual exploitation of children has become increasingly complex due to its trans-national scope. We know that children are sold and that there is traffic in children across frontiers; within Europe, from Asia to North and South America and from Asia to the Americas. It is a contemporary form of slavery, pervasive and expanding on many fronts. Furthermore the negative aspects of globalization facilitate its expansion. It is obvious, for example, that computer networks are being used to pass on information between abusers and traffickers and to disseminate child pornography worldwide. Some children are faced with an industry that lures them into exploitation. Sexual trade is spiralling towards the very young. While traditionally some customers believed that by resorting to young victims they would rejuvenate themselves, there is now the equally disturbing trend of believing that the selection of young victims offers protection against the HIV virus and Aids.

Child pornography
Child pornography, which is often linked with prostitution, can be defined as

'the visual or audio depiction of a child for the sexual gratification of the user, involving the production, distribution, and/or use of such material'. This definition also embraces pornographic performances. Examples of child pornography in practice are: parents making children appear in pornographic films; runaway children becoming models in order to earn their living; children being specially procured for pornography and prostitution; and parents (mostly mothers) themselves working as models in pornography and introducing their children into the industry. Child pornography is an area where the law has been overtaken to an extent by technology. There is evidence internationally of a shift away from difficult legal concepts such as obscenity and indecency. It is, however, often not easy to know where to draw the line precisely.

Prevalence of child prostitution
Information is fragmentary about the prevalence of child prostitution in Britain. National data is unavailable as is a national picture. It is likely, though, that hundreds of children are involved. We know that between 1989 and 1995 2,380 cautions were issued and 1,730 convictions were secured against those under eighteen in England and Wales. In 1996, according to the latest Home Office figures, 210 children were convicted of offences relating to prostitution compared to 101 children in 1995. The number of cautions rose slightly from 263 to 287. Included in the figures was the case of an eleven year old girl who was cautioned for an offence related to prostitution; she was the youngest person to be cautioned since 1992.

Who are the children involved in child prostitution? The Council of Europe's Report in 1993 refers to emotionally damaged children from broken homes, runaways, drug users and 'street children'. Studies in the United Kingdom point to young runaways and the connection with prostitution. The running away being from their own homes and from placements in care. The Children Society's 1994 study of young runaways reported on the experiences of young people who came into contact with street-work projects. A large majority ran away before the age of sixteen and one in seven had provided sex for money. Everyone preferred to refer to the experience as a 'survival strategy' rather than prostitution.

The 1994 study also referred to an apparently high incidence of cautioning and conviction of children under eighteen for prostitution. These were children who in other circumstances might have been subject to child protection procedures under the *Children Act 1989*. The Children Society's later publication in 1995, *The Game's Up*, provides further invaluable information. Where the courts are involved, those connected with cases involving child prostitution, and particularly judges and lawyers, will point to the almost invariable link with drugs. From other studies in the United Kingdom it would appear that young runaways from the care system in particular are at high risk of becoming involved in prostitution as a survival strategy and also of becoming involved in crime and with drugs. This is a specific and stark aspect that needs to be considered with the legal duties and responsibilities of local authorities under the *Children Act 1989* (and the *Children [Scotland] Act 1995)*. There is also a real problem with those who have recently left care because of their age. There is, in addition, increasing evidence to link childhood sexual abuse with prostitution and that the child is looking for an escape route. As David Barrett, a leading academic, has pointed out 'a perpetrator within a family may cause the young person to flee the family home to be exploited by other perpetrators. Although unusual some parents even 'work' their children as prostitutes.'

As a correct response to child prostitution, we must surely take on board the Council of Europe suggestions put forward in 1993. They concentrate on prevention first of all and targeting the high risk groups. The Report suggests the continuous and systematic control by social services and police of places that are likely to attract young prostitutes and their clients, such as stations, airports and seaports. Many recommendations are made including the involvement of mobile units of specialist social workers.

International law
In regard to the right response the law has, of course, a major role to play. From an international perspective, the most important legal instrument is the *UN Convention on the Rights of the Child* which was ratified by the UK Government in December 1991 (two months after the *Children Act 1989* was implemented). Over 190 countries have ratified the Convention, so it carries enormous persuasive authority. It is not part of our law in this country and there is no right of individual petition, as is the case with the *European Convention on Human Rights*. However, under Article 44 countries agree to report on the measures they have adopted which give effect to the rights recognised in the Convention and on the progress made in the enjoyment of those rights.

Article 19 is of great importance. Countries agree to take all appropriate legislative, administrative, social and educational measures to protect the child from all forms of physical or mental violence, injury or abuse, neglect or negligent treatment, maltreatment or exploitation, including sexual abuse while in anyone's care. Paragraph 2 of Article 19 states that such protective measures should, as appropriate, include effective procedures for the establishment of social programmes to provide necessary support for the child and for those who have the care of the child, as well as other forms of prevention; for identification, reporting, referral, investigation, treatment and follow-up of instances of child maltreatment and, as appropriate, for judicial involvement.

Article 34 provides that state parties undertake to protect the child from all forms of sexual exploitation and sexual abuse. For these purposes, (countries) shall take all appropriate....... measures to prevent:

- the inducement or coercion of a child to engage in any unlawful activity;
- the exploitative use of children in prostitution or other unlawful sexual practices;
- the exploitative use of children in pornographic performances and materials.

Article 35 deals with the prevention of the abduction, sale or trafficking in children for any purpose, while Article 39 provides for the promotion of the recovery and social reintegration of child victims.

There is a strong argument that this country is in breach of many parts of the Convention, which it should be remembered sets minimum standards. In January 1995 the UN Committee on the Rights of the Child seriously criticised the United Kingdom government. In particular there was criticism over the impact of some of its policies on children and young people. The Committee recommended that the issue of sexual exploitation of children should be addressed as a matter of urgency, with an emphasis on prevention. In addition, it was said that more effective strategies should be developed to promote the physical, psychological and social recovery of the child victim.

English civil and criminal law

What of our civil and criminal laws and particularly the child protection provisions of the *Children Act 1989?* Are they adequate and are they being applied properly and effectively? In short the answer, in my view, is that the *Children Act 1989* places sufficient duties on local authorities and adequate responsibilities are placed on them. The duties in the main, however, are not adequately undertaken. Regarding the criminal law, it is generally being used against children instead of being used against those who exploit them. In particular we should be using the civil law and not the criminal law in respect of children. The approach should be towards prevention. If that fails, protection not prosecution should be the policy.

Part 3 of the *Children Act 1989* provides for local authority support for children and families. Specific provisions place duties on the local authority to safeguard and promote the welfare of children within their area who are in need. A child is taken to be in need if, for example, his or her health or development is likely to be significantly impaired, or further impaired, without the provision for him or her of such services. Schedule 2 of the Act places a further range of duties on authorities. In particular, paragraph 7 of the Schedule provides that every local authority must take reasonable steps designed to reduce the need to bring criminal proceedings against children within their area. There are in fact a formidable and extensive range of provisions in the Act which should allow local authorities to intervene actively in order to do prevention work and divert children from prostitution. (See, for instance, sections 20, 31, 43, 44 and 47). The authorities are also often in a position to divert the police from using the criminal law as a response to child prostitution. The police, in cases of emergency, may under Section 46 remove a child to suitable accommodation and keep him or her there if the officer has reasonable cause to believe that a child would otherwise be likely to suffer significant harm.

I am quite convinced that the criminal law is not the answer to children involved in prostitution. It should be used against those who exploit and abuse children, and it should be used more creatively and energetically than it has been in the past. It may be that there is going to be a change in attitudes. Reviews and working parties may achieve this change. The criminal laws, the origins of which are in the last century, have developed piecemeal and without any obvious unifying principles. It is not surprising that they are complex, in places inconsistent, and in need of reform. The details are well set out in *The Game's Up* and are referred to in *Child Prostitution in Britain*, recently published by the Children's Society.

Conclusions
Overall, the following points may be made. Firstly, there needs to be wider recognition of the seriousness of the problem of child prostitution and the plight of the children exploited. Secondly, the approach towards the children should aim for protection not prosecution. Thirdly, the criminal law should not be used against children but against those who exploit and abuse them. Fourthly, in so far as the criminal law clashes with the civil law, the welfare approach should always prevail. Fifthly, there must be a multi-disciplinary approach to the protection of children, and sixthly, the government needs to reconsider its responsibilities under the UN Convention on the Rights of the Child as the criminalisation of children who are being sexually exploited is incompatible with the principles in the Convention.

There have been some hopeful signs recently. The Association of Directors of Social Services and the Association of Chief Police Officers have issued guidelines that state that children under sixteen who are found to be engaged in prostitution are to be dealt with in all circumstances under the *Children Act 1989*. In addition, it is said that the priority for the police will be the identification and prosecution of those offenders involved in the abuse of the child.

The problems, of course, will not be solved easily and they urgently need enlightened attention.

CHILDREN'S ADVOCACY CENTRES
An American model of response to inquiries into child sexual abuse

Sophie Hughes, Planning and Review Manager, Hereford Social Services

The Children's Advocacy Centre (CAC) movement in the United States aims to reduce trauma for alleged victims of child sexual abuse by cutting the risks of further damage caused by the inquiry process itself. Does it work? And if so, what can Britain learn from the CACs?

In essence, the CAC model aims for a focused, child-centred approach from the first moment of referral, carried through to every stage of the subsequent work. Centres, which have been created in a variety of locations bring the key players together in an environment specially designed to be child-friendly. There is strong emphasis on skilled forensic interviewing, medical examination, and individual support for the child. Practitioners from the police, prosecution, medical and social work services work as a team to create a response tailored to the individual needs of children who may have been abused. Specialist volunteers may play a significant role in the process of welcoming and supporting the child, and there is ready access to therapeutic services for the children and non-offending family members at all stages of the inquiry process.

CACs have been developed over the past ten years in response to a scenario similar to our own, pre-Cleveland, where children were subjected to multiple interviews and examinations, and were poorly supported through any following civil or criminal court proceedings. Centres modelled on the key principles of the movement are increasingly widespread in the USA, and a government sponsored national network and training programme supports their further development.

Miriam Wolf from Stuart House in Santa Monica, when speaking to an audience in Herefordshire, traced the original rationale for the movement. *We as practitioners recognised similarities between the behaviour of the system and that of the abuser. First we gained the children's confidence. Then we took what we wanted. Then we discarded them. The process of inquiry was publicly replicating the private experience of the abused child.*

In Britain many would recognise that, with the best of intentions and efforts at our disposal, this is too often the case in our own practice. Those children who have had the courage to speak of their own abuse will often, with hindsight, also speak of their regret that the working system itself seemed to undermine the healing process which it ought to have enabled.

CACs aim to change this radically, by providing an holistic response to the children and, crucially, the same team of workers who stick with each case throughout the process of enquiry. As well as offering a more healing experience for the child, there are additional spin-offs. Whereas in Britain prosecution rates for sexual offenders are falling, the CAC approach has contributed to a reverse trend in the States. Part of this is to do with gathering evidence robust enough to support a court case. In the words of Cathy Singletary, programme director of CAST, the State-run Centre in Orange County, *the children are more intact, more able to participate in the prosecution process, and make better witnesses.*

From the practitioners' vantage point, the multi-disciplinary approach provides an environment where skills can develop and creative technique can flourish. The concentration of expertise and experience means the teams attract community respect and high credibility within the justice system. In addition to their primary role, many centres act as sources of expertise for educational programmes in schools, colleges and the wider community. While not underestimating the intrinsic challenges of achieving a multi-disciplinary team approach, the purposeful attitude and high morale of professionals involved in the work of the centres is palpable.

Among other special skills needed to gain children's trust, the expertise of the medical examiner has become highly developed within the CAC movement. Jeanie Ming, nurse practitioner from CAST, speaks of a range of techniques designed to gain the child's confidence, always with the aim of relaxing, reassuring and empowering the child and family with accurate, sensitively delivered information and, where needed, appropriate follow-through. Video evidence is not permissible in the American court system, and the role of medical practitioner as expert witness consequently assumes a high profile.

A pivotal system difference between the two countries is the Americans' freedom to involve the District Attorney (DA), equivalent to our Crown Prosecutor, from the beginning stages of each enquiry. Whereas in Britain the Crown Prosecution Service (CPS) picks up cases some way along the line, remaining remote from front-line practice, in CACs the DA is part of the team and in some cases conducts the initial interview of the child in person.

Several key themes emerge and locally in Hereford an action plan is in the process of development. There is a strong view that closer involvement by the CPS could be achieved in Britain in order to improve transparency on the criteria influencing selection of cases for prosecution. Poor communication in this area has been identified by practitioners from all agencies as a source of frustration to themselves and of further damage and confusion to alleged victims.

More immediately attainable for British practitioners could be the simple but highly effective CAC strategy of identifying a named individual, sometimes a skilled volunteer, who stays with each case throughout the process, including standing alongside the child in the witness box should the case go to court. Such an individual can act as keyworker for the child and help the family through the often mystifying and drawn out process of getting (or not getting) a case to court.

Dr. Camille San Lazaro, Britain's only senior lecturer in paediatric forensic medicine, says that many core elements of the CAC model are common to her own practice in Newcastle. Out of 160 cases referred to her unit 57 alleged perpetrators reached trial and 49 were convicted.[i] This compares favourably with other parts of the country, where figures, though elusive, reveal that only small numbers of alleged perpetrators of abuse are charged or prosecuted, dwindling to virtually nil for cases involving children under the age of eight, She says there is no doubt that Britain is failing its children. While cautious about some aspects of the CAC approach, she is interested in the concept of a child advocate, saying that the child needs somebody who is an advocate for them at all sorts of levels and that social workers cannot always play that role. She believes we need an advocate who is truly independent and, who is not linked to the different disciplinary institutions.

i.   Dr C San Lazaro/A M Steele, *Outcome of criminal investigations into allegations of sexual abuse*, Archives of Diseases in Childhood, August 1996.

BEARING THE UNBEARABLE - WORKING WITH CHILD ABUSE

Dr. Roger Kennedy, Consultant Psychotherapist, The Cassel Hospital

What I mean by *Bearing the Unbearable* is that in the treatment of abused and abusing families, time and again the staff and the families are called upon to bear unbearable experiences, traumatically painful memories of abuse which the immature child cannot and could not deal with. By helping the children and their parents to bear these difficult experiences, to find words to express their distress, we hope to enable them to take charge of their lives, rather than continue to be victims of their past.

My own perspective comes from experience of working with the whole family at the Family Unit of the Cassel Hospital. The Unit is often used as a place of last resort for multi-problem families, many of whom have suffered from various forms of child physical, sexual and emotional abuse. Up to 14 families are admitted at any one time, initially for a six week assessment period, followed by the possibility of 12 to 18 months of intensive treatment.

Families live in the Unit for the week, depending upon circumstances and where they live. The Hospital is a seven-day facility, but we encourage families to remain in contact with their home community - though many of our families have few local contacts anyway, and are often socially isolated. In families who are undergoing rehabilitation, where they may be coming together after the children have been removed and are still in foster care, it may take some months before they are finally reunited. Until that point, children may have to return to foster care for most weekends, until a gradual rehabilitation programme is completed.

Treatment consists of a combination of intensive psychoanalytic psychotherapy, group and family therapy, and nursing work focused around everyday family life. Everyday issues - what I call the *Work of the Day* - become the focus of the nursing work, such as getting up in the morning, going to bed, eating together, most of which have often broken down in these families. It is the particular combination of the nursing and therapy that is unique to the Cassel.

Listening to the abused child
It is worth adding here that this may include on occasions being alert to the fact

that some children are abusers of other children. The children at the Cassel often seem at first haunted by their abuse and are unable to free themselves from its consequences without considerable help. As others have repeatedly observed, such children often show a number of pathological features. For example, they may be unable to concentrate on a task for long, appear over-stimulated with poor impulse control, which may make it difficult to listen to them, and they have a haunted, driven quality in their relating, with a tendency to be aggressive and testing of boundaries. They sometimes show inappropriate sexual behaviour; may go in and out of confusional states when they become very anxious, particularly about being abandoned; they have difficulty trusting in adults; they become intrusive and irritating in their behaviour. The parent-child relationships are usually pathological, with varying degrees of disorganised attachments. There is often role reversal, in which the children try to control the parent and are over-solicitous, while the parents have problems in maintaining ordinary child-adult boundaries. The children may have a buildup of emotional tension with which the parent cannot deal, which then leads to an outburst of frustration and despair. These episodes may be accompanied by the projection of primitive fantasies between child and adult, in which there is a mix-up of child and adult elements. Working with the whole family necessitates taking up these issues vigorously, and helping the parent and child find a safer distance between them.

Working with the parents
A frequent simple finding in the parents is that they consistently show great difficult in being emotionally attached to their children, with inhibition of the capacity to play. They are often inconsistent, at times cut off and self-absorbed. Suicidal feelings in them may be triggered by the threat of experiencing vulnerability. Acting rather then understanding is a common means of communicating for both parents and children, which often makes the treatment very demanding and at times exhausting for professionals. This is particularly the case when the staff have to be the ones who feel the child's pain and vulnerability for the parent. There often seems to be a need for the children to make a particular kind of emotional impact on their parents and other caretakers, especially when the parents are impervious to the child's emotional needs. The children may be trying desperately to get the parents to acknowledge their needs, while also attacking them for having failed them. Of course, many of the abusing parents have also been abused as children, which makes it difficult for them to experience the child's pain. When they try to put themselves in the child's shoes, they feel as if they themselves are the abused child, and they may cut off from being in contact with the child. Our research shows, however, that adults who have had abusing experiences in childhood but can develop a capacity for self-reflection in therapy can more effectively deal with their own abuse, and can be safer with their children.

Helping the professional

Clearly, working with the abusing and abused family is difficult work and not everyone can do this. One has to be both sensitive to the families yet also resilient enough to help them bear unbearable experiences. Confusion, anger and helplessness are common experiences in professionals involved in this work. However, clear lines of professional responsibility, effective communication between workers and the attempt to provide an atmosphere in which trust between workers and the families develops can help to deal with these inevitable strains. Also essential is ongoing and experienced supervision of front-line staff by senior staff, as well as sharing of strains with other workers. At the same time, it is an inevitable and necessary part of the work to withstand considerable amounts of destructive behaviour from the families. Workers may take unhelpful attitudes towards the families instead of clearly focusing on the issues. For example, workers may either collude with difficulties and play them down, or alternatively have too negative a view of them. Supervision may be needed to tease out what belongs to the family and what belongs to the professional and the professional team.

PART TWO

PRACTICAL DIFFICULTIES ENCOUNTERED BY POLICE, PROBATION AND SOCIAL SERVICES; THE KEY ISSUES FOR INTER-AGENCY WORKING WITHIN THE *SEX OFFENDERS ACT 1997*

**Alan Bowman, Director of Social Services, Brighton & Hove Council;
Penny Buller, Chief Probation Officer, East Sussex;
Mike Lewis, Sussex Police; George Smith, Sussex Police**

Introduction: Mike Lewis
The aim of this presentation is to outline the practical difficulties faced by the three agencies - police, probation and social services - in dealing with Robert Oliver, a high profile convicted paedophile, by giving an overview of his case from three perspectives within the risk assessment group in Brighton. In so doing, it is important to recognise that we are dealing with a case that is still 'live', as colleagues elsewhere are still dealing with the case. We must remember that the subject of our case study is a free man; he has served his sentence and our close involvement with him has been entirely as a result of his request for assistance.

The Oliver Case: George Smith
At 2.15 pm on Thursday 9th October, 1997 I received a telephone call from a colleague in the Midlands informing me that Robert Oliver was on a train travelling to Brighton due to arrive at 8.45 pm. At that time my knowledge of Oliver was very limited. I faintly recalled media interest about his release from prison. During the next couple of hours our telephone and fax lines were kept busy as we endeavoured to find out more about this individual. We established:

- that Robert Francis Oliver was born on the 2nd October, 1954;
- that on the 15th May, 1989 Robert Oliver had been sentenced at the Central Criminal Court to 15 years imprisonment for manslaughter for his part in a sex ring involving the abduction and killing of 14 year old Jason Swift. The original charge was murder;
- that Oliver had been released from HMP Wandsworth on the 26th September, 1997;
- that Oliver was not under any supervision order. He had been assessed in prison as 'extremely high risk' with regard to the possibility of his committing further offences against young boys.

Because of media interest and a public demonstration, Oliver did not stay at the planned address in London. He went to Swindon, where he was identified by the media, and Wiltshire Police named him under the *Sex Offenders Act, 1997*. Under this Act he was registered in Swindon.

Oliver then returned to a hostel in London, but was made unwelcome there, so travelled to Holyhead and caught the ferry to Dublin. The Garda, who had been alerted, detained him in cells for five hours and put him back on the ferry to Liverpool. From there Oliver went directly to Manchester and was met by the local police. Following an overnight stay officers put him on the Manchester to Brighton train. He had only ever been to Brighton on one day trip in about 1982 and had no known contacts in the town. He was due to arrive at Brighton that Thursday evening, within a couple of hours of our knowing. We were being presented with a difficult problem which was not of our making.

From the outset the safety of the community was our priority. It required a professional and responsible approach. We needed to establish if he had arrived in the town and where he was staying, so an operation was quickly pulled together. When Oliver arrived his movements were closely monitored and at all times we knew where he was. He spent his first night in town at a local hostel. On the Friday the police called a risk assessment conference, together with probation and social services. As a temporary measure, it was agreed that close police monitoring would continue over the weekend and that a detective inspector would visit him at the hostel to let him know we knew he was in town. It was agreed the meeting would reconvene on the Monday.

Even in October, Brighton is a busy seaside town with hundreds of unsupervised children on the pier and in amusement arcades. Their safety was paramount. During Friday evening Oliver met up with a well known local convicted paedophile and spent the night with him. He did not go back to the hostel and we decided that the detective inspector should not approach him. On Saturday Oliver met up with a man and they visited the Hove Library, where they spent much time in the children's section. Oliver spent that night at the local night shelter. On Sunday, still with the same man, he spent much of the day on the seafront, watching children playing. He again spent the night at the night shelter. His actions caused concern, but he had not committed a criminal offence.

Early on the Monday D.I. John May visited the shelter and spoke with Oliver. May let Oliver know that the police were aware of his presence in the town and robustly warned him that he would be closely monitored. He was told not to go near where children played. In Monday's edition of a national newspaper a story with photographs of Oliver appeared, with the headline *Where is this fiend?* It encouraged its readers to ring a hot-line if they knew where the 'fiend' was living. A second risk assessment conference was held at Brighton Police Station on the Monday, with the education authority also being invited. During the meeting the police public relations office was informed that the press had been told Oliver had travelled from Manchester and had been in Brighton for a week. They were asked what the police were doing about it and why had the public not been warned?

Following agreement with Assistant Chief Constable Wallis a joint press release was issued. The press release confirmed Oliver was in town and stressed that we were aware of the fact and had been closely monitoring his movements from the outset. Again, a principle concern had been the safety of the community. In addition, the education authority issued a letter to schools naming Oliver. On the next day, the 14th October, major articles appeared in the national newspapers and on television. There was intense and persistent media interest.

At 11.30 am on that Tuesday, a joint police/social services press conference was held, fronted by D.C.C. Jordan. Public reassurance was the principle issue. During the Tuesday afternoon the police station was inundated with telephone calls from concerned and irate members of the public. The crime desk was dealing with over 40 calls an hour and the main switchboard had difficulty dealing with the volume. People also came to the police station to complain and there were persistent calls from the media. By about 2.30 pm the media had identified the night shelter and people descended there, making enquiries of staff and neighbours. There were also reporters roaming the town, offering money for details of the whereabouts of Oliver. The director of the shelter said that because of the intense media attention they could no longer accommodate him. Oliver had no money and no likelihood of accommodation. He had not committed any offence, but was associating with known sex offenders. It was considered unsafe to allow him to wander the streets and simply to disappear. The principle object was to maintain contact and know his whereabouts. D.I. May approached him and Oliver asked for help, whereupon Oliver was taken to the police station.

A meeting was called by the police that evening. It quickly became apparent that neither probation nor housing could realistically offer local accommodation to Oliver. For several hours Penny Buller and I telephoned and pleaded with numerous institutions, agencies and charities for temporary accommodation, but none could assist. Late that Tuesday evening the police decided, with Oliver's agreement, to accommodate him in a small police station out of Brighton, as a place of safety. A uniformed officer remained with him. Oliver was to remain with us for four long months.

The intensity of interest from the media and public was far greater than any murder investigation I have known and the commitment actually to dealing with the issue was on a par with the first hectic days of a major crime investigation. It was the first time in my career that I have addressed a demonstration outside the police station. I also received hate mail from people who considered we were protecting him.

On a practical note, from the beginning I had documented every message, contact and policy agreement. The key players were issued with a folder and each received a copy of all documentation. This worked very effectively and reduced the chance of confusion. The main press line was that we had a difficult problem, which we were jointly endeavouring to resolve, and that the safety of the public remained our priority. The police provided the place of safety because we preferred to know where Oliver was, rather than have him roaming the country.

Key Issues for the Police: Mike Lewis
Media pressure
The media pressure in those first few days was relentless and deflected the risk assessment group from its primary purpose of trying to resolve how best to protect the community in Brighton and to meet the needs of Robert Oliver. Once we were able to satisfy the media and the community that Oliver no longer presented a threat, then the focus - certainly of the broadsheets - shifted to what we felt was a more helpful position, in that they raised the debate nationally about the issues presented by the Oliver case. It is fair to say, however, that during those four months there were literally daily enquiries from the media.

Surveillance capacity
Many observers, indeed many communities, have an expectation that police can put individuals under surveillance for extended periods. The reality, as police colleagues will appreciate, is that surveillance is an extremely costly operational tool and that the capacity within most forces is very limited. In Sussex the requirement to place a high risk individual under surveillance for any extended period would certainly impact significantly on other police operations and, frankly, could not be sustained.

Attitude of staff and families
Maintaining an element of secrecy over the location of Oliver's 'place of safety' was critical to the risk assessment group whilst we sought more appropriate accommodation. We were anxious not to put local officers under unnecessary pressure from the media, nor local communities. We were aware when the local media became aware of his location, but were grateful that they chose not to divulge it. The greatest potential for a leak was from within and we were aware that a number of officers and their partners questioned whether 'guarding' an individual such as Oliver was appropriate.

Lay visitor
One of the safeguards that we built in to our 'place of safety' arrangements was

to invite an independent lay visitor to satisfy the risk assessment group that Oliver was being housed with his agreement and that his personal requirements were being met. We would commend such arrangements to others.

Risk assessment group
It is importance to maintain continuity within the risk assessment group and, as far as practicable, to keep the same players around the table for the duration. All the work within the risk assessment group was locally based in Brighton, albeit with the full knowledge and support of chief officers at headquarters. Given the national profile of the case, however, it was necessary to bring in chief officers at key stages; it is important to recognise how this can potentially imbalance the risk assessment group and how channels of communication might be strained.

The Police Authority
I have just referred to the national profile of what we were doing and of course the local interest was intense. It was vital therefore that, from the police perspective, we kept the Police Authority in the picture from the start; we needed to be confident that we had their support in what we were trying to achieve. This was not a question of undermining the chief constable's 'operational independence'; that was never the issue. It was about reassuring local communities, through the Police Authority, that we were acting professionally and in the best interests of all parties. The Authority's support was unequivocal, but was never intrusive. I remember well the chairman, a local Brighton councillor, saying 'don't tell me where he is, it is better for me not to know'. That confidence in what we were doing was important and the Authority continues to play a key role in taking the debate forward.

As a divisional commander, I was also anxious to ensure that key individuals locally - e.g. the chair of the Police Consultation and Public Safety Committee - were properly briefed on the issues and our approach, whilst maintaining confidentiality.

The Role of the Probation Service: Penny Buller
1.   Setting the context
I had been away at a conference when Robert Oliver arrived in Brighton and initially the case was handled by an Assistant Chief Probation Officer. I returned to my office on Monday, 13 October, four days after Mr Oliver's arrival in the area. I found on my desk a message from my colleague, who had by then started a period of leave, saying 'URGENT - this case may blow'. Little did I know, at that stage, the extent of the explosion which was to follow. We had virtually no information about Robert Oliver. He had been released from prison at his non-parole date and without statutory supervision by the probation service, so there

was no 'case file'. There were no details available at that stage of the circumstances of his offence, his previous convictions, his progress in custody or a recent risk assessment. We were essentially starting from scratch. Lessons to be learned from these beginnings are:

- The need to identify 'notorious/high profile' offenders who are likely to become a media target prior to release, in order to have available a comprehensive dossier of up-to-date information which can be accessed by any area to which they go after release. This would need to be co-ordinated nationally, with a central register which receiving areas could check.
- A crisis never comes at a convenient time! (My Assistant Chief, who should have dealt with it, went on leave!) It is essential to identify one 'lead' person to manage the case and with the authority to take decisions in collaboration with the other agencies.
- It is impossible to know how long such a crisis may last. None of us ever, in our wildest dreams, thought that Robert Oliver would sit in a police station in Sussex, for four months. However, continuity of personnel is important and will require re-ordering of priorities and commitments, possibly for a protracted period.

2.   Managing a crisis
By Tuesday, 14th October, Robert Oliver had requested sanctuary and Sussex Police had taken him, as a temporary measure, into a police station as a 'place of safety'. At the inter-agency meeting that evening there were two priorities:

- finding suitable, safe accommodation for him;
- maintaining confidentiality in the face of growing press interest.

We pooled ideas as there were no helpful precedents to work from and no convenient lists of possible placement options. We phoned around but nowhere could/would take him as an emergency. The one probation managed hostel in Sussex is located on the seafront in Brighton and was deemed unsuitable, as unaccompanied young people abound in the area, and also because the press would be likely to find him almost immediately and provoke public reaction. Many of the voluntary hostels already had sex offender residents and were, understandably, fearful of press intrusion. The Wolvercote Centre in Surrey, which specialises in the treatment of sex offenders was approached, but does not take residents without a full assessment as to suitability.

As we grew more desperate, and as the evening lengthened, we even considered rural religious retreats; in fact, anywhere which might give us a breathing space in which to find a long-term solution. We drew a complete blank until, finally,

Sussex Police agreed to continue to accommodate Mr Oliver (with his consent) for the next few days. It is important to remember that his was a controversial decision at the time. We were all too aware that it was very far from ideal and raised civil liberties issues. It may now, with the wisdom of hindsight, seem an obvious and pragmatic response, but on that evening we were all concerned about it.

The following day, Wednesday, 15th October, produced intense media interest. Work in planning for Mr Oliver's future was constantly disrupted by the arrival of press on the doorstep and continual telephone enquiries and the like. The probation service in the area has no press department, as our one public relations officer had been made redundant due to budget cuts the previous year. Although Sussex Police handled the brunt of the media, probation was by no means exempt and it was crucial that we, the police and social services had an agreed strategy for what we could, and would not, say. A joint press conference was held that afternoon.

Trying to focus on a solution for Mr Oliver was a priority. Surveillance by the police while he was at large in Brighton provided invaluable intelligence that he remained a risk to children and young people. Staff from the probation service with specialist training in work with sex offenders conducted a risk assessment on Mr Oliver, and we also called in the forensic psychiatrist from the regional secure unit to conduct an assessment. There was unanimity in assessing him as a high risk in terms of future offending. Lessons to be learned from handling the crisis are:

- The need to learn from others' experience as cases such as these multiply. The purpose of this seminar is to disseminate such experience otherwise each case will involve 'reinventing the wheel'.
- The importance of established working relations between the relevant agencies. Agreed protocols on confidentiality, information sharing, co-working etc. are very helpful, although it is not until they are put to the test in a crisis that their real value is tested.
- The need for an agreed press strategy with clearly defined responsibilities and explicit decisions about what will and will not be released. Working with the press can be enormously time-consuming, but may pay dividends. Equally it may prove frustrating and counter-productive, especially with the tabloids.

3.   The long haul
Over the next four months, while Mr Oliver remained in a police cell, innumerable attempts were made to place him. My own opinion was that he required a high level of security in order to monitor him and protect the public from further

offending. This view was shared by the police and social services locally. Outside the prison system, the most secure accommodation was to be found in the special hospitals and I felt that this was the most appropriate placement. Specialists from Broadmoor and Rampton assessed him, but felt that he did not fall within the criteria of the *Mental Health Act*. Even if he had been assessed as having a condition such as psychopathy within the meaning of the Act, there were doubts about treatability. Sexual deviance per se, regardless of dangerousness, is specifically excluded from the Act. We were unable to place him in a secure psychiatric unit or a special hospital despite numerous referrals to both NHS and private hospitals.

The other (in my view less satisfactory) option was some form of hostel placement. I had reservations about the level of monitoring and surveillance which would be possible, but one voluntary organisation was prepared to consider a placement and began to put extra physical security measures (for example pressure pads, video cameras) into one of its properties. However, at the eleventh hour this placement was withdrawn and we were back to square one.

Contact with civil servants in the Home Office had, initially, been less than helpful. We were told that the case was a local, operational matter rather than a national issue. We were also told that there was no central funding for any placement. Accommodation of the sort we believed to be essential for public protection was inevitably going to be expensive. There was no 'responsible authority' prepared to fund a placement. Indeed, we considered it simply happenstance that Mr Oliver had come to Sussex. He had no ties in the area and had never been resident there. Over the months, due in no small part to political pressure, civil servants did try to help, but the funding issue remains unresolved.

Mr Oliver is now at a private medium-secure unit in another part of the country. He is there for a limited period to be assessed. We still have no long-term placement and no funding for him. He is not the only case of his kind. There are about 150 more sex offenders in prison, sentenced before the *Criminal Justice Act 1991*, who, if they do not get parole, will be released without supervision. A handful are as dangerous and notorious as Robert Oliver. One of them could turn up in your area, you could be next; it is vital that, together, we learn the lessons and arrive at better solutions than are currently available. Lessons to be learned from the long haul are:

- A review of the *Mental Health Act* criteria is needed to assess whether this very small group of personality disordered, dangerous paedophiles could/ should be detained in a psychiatric setting.
- It must be accepted that this small group poses a national problem. They could arrive anywhere with no warning, or move from place to place. National

co-ordination is needed and, in my opinion, national funding is needed for placements and this is bound to be expensive. It is not right for a local area to bear the brunt of long-term funding for someone who is not a resident.

- Extended supervision of sex offenders by the probation service, as contained in the *Crime and Disorder Bill*, is no panacea. It will locate responsibility more clearly, but without the availability of suitable accommodation for this group it will be a nightmare for any probation officer to hold the supervision.
- Local inter-agency working can be as excellent as you like, but these cases go beyond the local remit. There needs to be similar inter-departmental co-operation nationally, with a national task force to oversee and fund what, I repeat, are a small number of notorious and dangerous sex offenders.

Local Authority Perspective and Responsibilities: Alan Bowman
In looking at the local authority's role, I will focus primarily on social services, whose key responsibility is the protection of children and young people. In cases other than Oliver's, where issues of mental health, age and infirmity or disability are a factor, we would have other responsibilities and duties which might allow us to intervene proactively in other ways. In this case there was no basis for these forms of intervention, albeit that Oliver was likely to be homeless and that his presence might give rise to issues of community safety, as well as touch on other responsibilities of the local authority.

Political liaison
Given the considerable coverage in the media which has been referred to earlier, it was important that local politicians be kept as fully informed of the developing situation as possible. This meant briefing elected members of the Council and also local Members of Parliament. One interesting benefit for us was that two Members of Parliament were still elected members of the Council and the leader of our Council had recently been appointed as a working peer by the Government. Our key objectives in providing information to local politicians were, firstly, to keep them informed appropriately and to ensure they were fully briefed in the event that they may be required to make a response to the media. Secondly, to ensure that any response was consistent and accurate. Our third objective was to enlist the support of local Members of Parliament in pressing the Government to assist us in managing the difficult problem. How did we do this and what has been the outcome?

We first decided that there was a need to ensure early and accurate communication regarding the situation and the steps being taken to manage it. That was followed rapidly by a series of regular face-to-face briefing meetings, which allowed matters to be discussed much more fully. Again it was important, in the context of these meetings, to demonstrate the degree of inter-agency cooperation. During the course of these meetings we were able to identify and reach agreement on those areas where local politicians could take action and not take action. What was striking throughout this process was the degree of commitment from Members of Parliament in helping us resolve this difficult situation and the considerable efforts they were prepared to make, both in terms of lobbying and other action, to ensure there was an effective outcome. Through this process, we achieved a consistent, measured approach locally. There was raised political awareness of this difficult issue and also of the wider implications of managing such cases. The efforts of local Members of Parliament in lobbying ministers certainly assisted the immediate resolution of the case. There is to be a final meeting between Members of Parliament, ministers and senior officers to look at the management of the case and the wider issues that flow from it. All in all, the political contribution to managing this difficult situation has been particularly effective and it is important that national and local political strategies are in harmony, rather than conflict, on this matter.

Information
The impact of media coverage runs throughout the management of this case. As part of the risk assessment process, clear decisions need to be taken about how much information can appropriately be shared with particular individuals or agencies. In the case of Robert Oliver, the local director of education and I issued a letter to the parents of all school children and also to all childminders, foster carers and other agencies looking after children in Brighton and Hove. The purpose of that letter was twofold; first to alert and to remind families of the risks posed to children by Robert Oliver and others but, more importantly, to demonstrate to parents that we had taken control of a difficult situation, were not shirking our responsibilities and that they should have confidence in us and leave us to deal with the matter. This was particularly important as the anxiety and concern being whipped up by increasingly alarmist media reports, was clearly causing distress across the whole community. We have had excellent feedback on this letter, which seems to have been well received across the whole community. It would be unlikely that without the kind of media coverage that accompanied the Oliver case, it would be necessary to take such action. There may, however, be a case for more localised information in respect of particular offenders and particular communities, but these are the kind of judgements that can only be made within the risk assessment group. What is actually to be done will be governed by the individual circumstances of any case.

Managing the media
Much of our time during the handling of this case has been concerned with managing the media and recognising the significant level of interest in this matter.

From the outset, we sought to present a united front both through press conferences, interviews and press releases. Inevitably, our efforts in this regard were tested considerably by the press and media, but generally during this reactive phase our objectives were largely achieved. At the same time, however, it was important to remember that the Oliver case was the local manifestation of a national problem; briefing of the press on the wider issues and contributing information to articles and programmes on radio and television was intended to secure a more measured and more thoughtful analysis of the problem. Again, this has been fairly successful, but it is also essential to the development of any national strategy for managing such cases. On a simple practical level our joint approach has, I believe, also worked to reassure the public. One brief comment I would make is that it was clear that Sussex Police have very good arrangements for managing high profile cases and it was very helpful for me to be able to work within their arrangements. This is a matter that should be considered locally, but it does seem sensible to make use of 'tried and tested' arrangements rather than create new ones.

Finally, I wish to conclude my contribution by returning to the input of local politicians. As we gradually moved towards some form of interim solution to the problem of Robert Oliver, it was clear that their efforts and lobbying in informing the ministers and in supporting at local and national level the actions we were taking, were of immense assistance. I think this highlights the point I made earlier about the need for speedy communication with local politicians, with frequent face to face briefings and clear agreement in the sharing of information on the action being taken by each individual.

Conclusion: Mike Lewis

In drawing this presentation to a conclusion, I hope that we have been able to highlight many of the practical difficulties facing our local risk assessment group in dealing with the Oliver case. Each of the agencies has identified key issues that emerged as a result of our joint working. Some are clearly agency-specific, such as the issue of police surveillance capacity. Many, such as the media issues, were shared. Four points bear particular emphasis:

Civil liberties

As I stated at the outset, we are here discussing a 'live' issue. Robert Oliver has served his sentence, he is not under license and he is not under supervision. At all times we were mindful of his civil liberties and his ability, as a free man, to walk out of his 'place of safety' at any time. A very real part of our frustration has been in trying to place an individual who wants to be helped.

Media pressure

The notoriety factor, described by Penny Buller as the 'demonisation factor', put each of the agencies under intense pressure in the early stages and was clearly a factor in making our search for suitable accommodation more difficult. Colleagues in another force, faced with a similar high profile case, acknowledge that an individual subject to the 'notoriety factor' in their area is not the most dangerous individual on their register of offenders, but is the most problematic because of the media interest. Colleagues should not underestimate the impact of that pressure.

Public safety

Throughout this episode, our primary consideration at all times has been the protection of vulnerable groups within the local community and that remains our priority.

Joint working

It goes without saying that joint working is essential with the risk assessment group. Well established protocols, developed long before the Oliver case, allowed us to come together quickly and to understand each other's perspectives and operational constraints. Colleagues may wish to reflect on their own situations locally. Flexibility is the key and I feel we enjoyed the confidence of each other in taking matters forward. It was genuinely a joint response, with no agency having overall precedence and that is vital.

Finally, in making this presentation, we are not offering our response as the model for dealing with similar cases. What we sought to do was adopt a professional approach to a very real issue; how to deal with an individual deemed a high risk who was being pursued relentlessly from place to place. Each time he moved the risk increased, in our assessment. Oliver need not have been a Sussex problem - but we felt that enough was enough. What we did in Brighton in offering a 'place of safety' to Oliver was only ever intended as an interim solution, but it was one with which we wrestled locally for over four months. Both this case, and the underlying issues, remain largely unresolved.

The two questions we would ask are these:

- At what stage does a local operational difficulty become a national issue, requiring central support and direction? Who actually owns the problem?

    and

- Will the next Oliver scenario be different?

ASSESSING RISK AND DANGEROUSNESS; PROBLEMS FOR THE POLICE IN OPERATING THE REGISTER

Ray Wyre, Independent Consultant

Not long ago a police officer discovered the body of a naked child on the beach. The first thing the officer did was to cover the body with his blue coat - and I think every one of us would understand the feelings that led him to take that action. However, by allowing his feelings to overrule his professional judgement, he contaminated the scene of the crime and made the crime more difficult to investigate.

In some ways this is also a metaphor for how we in society deal with abuse. Whenever we are confronted or challenged by abuse our tendency is to run and cover it up. We do not want to face the pain of what it is all about, which is why it is very difficult at times for us to listen and to translate those feelings into positive action. How many more horror stories do we have to hear before we actually implement policies that get the changes we need? When are we going to start treating the victims of abuse within our residential establishments, rather than just putting more children into such places to become future victims?

I am here to talk about the registration of sex offenders. Many people such as myself have been calling for a register for years and have been saying that we need a comprehensive register containing all known convicted sex offenders, including those who have appeared in civil proceedings. These offenders are a social work nightmare as they move from county to county, from family to family. If we can put children on a child protection register, why can we not put the people who abuse on a register as well? We also wanted to add to the list all those charged with professional misconduct, as well as others appearing on lists such as 'List 99', operated by local education authorities We also called for the development of a pin number for professionals working with children so that anyone appointed to a position would have their pin number checked for anything recorded or registered against them. This would solve the problem we often have of people changing their names by Deed Poll and would make it compulsory that those who do so be registered under their new name. Instead, a policy was introduced of registering those convicted of sex offences. Worse, it was only made applicable to those who worked subject to the statutory provisions of 1st September 1997 with the result that the 210,000 convicted sex offenders who are in the community, having been sentenced prior to 1993, are not subject to or part of that register. Civil proceedings were also excluded, so right from the beginning there were obvious criticisms that could be made.

We already had a register of convicted sex offenders operated by the police, so what is this register all about? The main problem lies in how we define sexual crime. For example, a man who abducts and kills a child is not subject to being placed on the register unless he has sexually abused that child. A man who tortures a child and is charged with manslaughter would not be subject to the register unless there were a proven sexual element to the crime. There were fundamental mistakes made in the creation of the register and these will need to be rectified if the register is going to be effective. As some of you will know, anyone sentenced for a sexual offence before 1991 is not subject to supervision on release, unless subject to parole. Robert Oliver is a prime example, but there are hundreds due to come out of prison, who were sent there before 1991, for whom no one will have statutory responsibility. However, these offenders will be obliged to register, giving the police a nightmare problem, because technically no-one has responsibility for those men; yet the police are meant to establish risk, to monitor and do a whole range of things.

The other problem we have is that people get sent to prison for what they are convicted of and not for their dangerousness. We all have very dangerous offenders with whom we work who may be on very low sentences, yet these sentences are also being used to decide how long people should be placed on the register. We have some sex offenders on probation who never go to prison, so those issues need to be looked at. We all know of offenders who are having to be released. When I worked in prison I used to recommend parole, not because these people were low risk but because I did not want them coming out into the community with no supervision at all. Thankfully that has been changed, except for the offenders sentenced before 1991, which is farcical because these are the most dangerous offenders of all.

We also have a problem with the criminal legislation dealing with mental health; the mad/bad debate continues. We still have the vast majority of sex offenders being dealt with by the criminal justice system, with psychiatrists mainly saying sex offending is a personality disorder and not amenable to treatment. This is convenient, but does not help us in what we do with the sexual offender, especially as most of these are in the community. Tied in with this is the wide range of behaviour that a person can get up to before you can do anything with them. In fact, not far from here a man was preparing to abduct a child. The police broke cover and moved in quickly, but they moved in before he had actually done anything, leaving the problem of how you do something within criminal law if you lack the evidence.

The other problem is community notification. I know there are some here who believe in community notification, but I have a major problem with it because of what the community does when it is told. Those of us running treatment programmes for sex offenders can find an offender in our group being chased out of town to a place where they are unknown and where the authorities have no real knowledge of them. We still have a major problem with how we define and how we decide - who should be notified. Managing risk in the community is always going to be a problem, mainly because of how society sees the sex offender. The sex offender is seen as a dangerous monster, an abductor, a person who is going to rape and kill a child - yet the reality is that this is a remote possibility - and present legislation and registration does not deal with that offender adequately anyway. If that offender is motivated to abuse he will go wherever he can get access to children, irrespective of whatever registration is in place. Looking at those children who were abducted and killed between 1984 - 88 we have a figure of 82. Looking again at those figures, and asking where the danger lay, we find that relatives and parents killed 76 children; only six were killed by strangers. Similar figures are available up to 1993, yet there is a fear in the community that somehow it is the sex offender who is going to abduct and kill. These figures are still too high, but nothing within our legislation is going to deal with that group and this means that I have to say something quite negative. Whatever we do, we must remember that there will always be those who are motivated to abuse and who will do so whatever systems we have in place. Whatever method of registration, supervision, treatment and monitoring we have, there is a duty for us to do whatever we can to reduce and manage the risk, otherwise future victims will have paid for the failure of our systems. Registers alone do not protect anyone; it is what you do with them that counts. I am sick of registers and protocols that are not delivering the service.

Let us look at what public vilification of sex offenders in America and Canada has done and what it is about. This vilification appears to have grown because of the problems in the management of information systems which were set up to monitor convicted sex offenders. If we as professionals cannot do the work, we cannot then complain when communities want to take matters into their own hands, irrespective of the fact that all the studies demonstrate that community notification does not reduce risk. Registration by itself does not reduce the risk of sex offending. The American experience would suggest that sound information management is essential in protecting the public from sex offenders. Effective management of the information by the relevant agencies is most important. In Los Angeles, in 1994, a child went missing. They have had a register there for many years and it was decided to check on the addresses of 4,400 registered sex offenders. Of the addresses checked, 90% were inaccurate. It is too easy to hide behind registers and not to look at what we should do if we are to manage sex offenders in the community.

What we have to recognise is that most child protection is *not* child protection, because people motivated to abuse are going to abuse; if the statutory agencies get their checking right the offender will move to voluntary agencies, and if the voluntary agencies check successfully offenders will then set up groups in their own homes. Failing that, these people will probably go to other countries where it is easier to abuse. Therefore, the most effective way forward, in my opinion, is to develop treatment programmes within the community and within institutions to reduce the risk of some of these people reoffending.

We also need to look at the role of the probation service in supervision. We are giving the service some of the most dangerous men, some of whom are not going to stop abusing, and it is the probation service which will be blamed when things fail. In the past the most dangerous people were not on parole and therefore nobody could be blamed when they reoffended. We are now holding people accountable, but are often not giving them the resources, nor giving them the legislation, they need to deal effectively with the problem they have been given. This also includes the development of relaxed prevention programmes, including telephone support lines.

Indeterminate sentencing also needs to be looked at. At the moment sex offenders can be detained in mental health facilities on a life sentence only as long as mental illness has been proved. Perhaps there is a way of developing indeterminate treatment programmes within the criminal justice system, but I remain unsure of how we can solve the problem. We need to introduce imaginative sentencing that recognises the problem of dangerousness. A man recently came to us for four weeks residential assessment. We realised how very dangerous he was and wanted him to come back into treatment. The probation service could not find adequate provision, the mental health authorities said he was not their problem as did social services and we had to let him go. He was initially put under police surveillance and his car was stopped on the motorway, because the police heard he was going to kill. It was too late; he already had a body in the boot of the car.

These dangerous offenders and the question of dangerousness should not take us away from the fact that the vast majority of sexual offenders do not operate like this. Unfortunately the media highlights these offenders in an attempt to stop us working with the vast majority of sex offenders, whose risk can be reduced through intensive work. We need to develop institutions where there can be intensive treatment within the criminal justice system. It seems that we would rather have sex offenders living anonymously in bedsits, than set up appropriate intensive programmes for them. Appropriate housing includes supervised housing. It has been said that offenders in unstable circumstances are likely to commit further offences and that agencies should cooperate to ensure that stable accommodation is available for offenders on discharge. It is a farcical and dangerous policy that leads to some housing organisations saying they will not have sex offenders in their housing. This just means that they have to be put in bedsits and bed and breakfast houses, where the only other occupants are single parents with children. We must recognise that sex offenders are in the community and need to be housed, so we must look at relevant supervised housing for some of them.

The other problem we have is that there is an expectation that the police will assess risk. I have been working for years attempting to assess risk with sex offenders and it is a nightmare, yet overnight we are suddenly asking untrained police to assess risk. Risk assessment is a difficult task and the police are having to depend on other agencies to assist them in their task. All 43 police areas are developing their own protocols and networks. The register was introduced without discussion with all the agencies and I know that many areas have now got together to look at risk patterns. Some ideas have come up with regard to helping the police assess risk, including the concept of one point = low risk, two - three points = medium risk, four plus points = high risk. It is a very practical way of trying to assess the risk of some sex offenders present in the community.

Having assessed risk, what are you going to do with the knowledge? You cannot take offenders back into custody and the mental health legislation is not going to be used to take them off the streets. Are you going to use surveillance? With some abusers of children you would have to watch them for a year before they actually did anything for which they could be charged and convicted. We therefore have to look at recommendations that have come out of various reports. Disciplinary action should not be circumvented so as to lead to resignation. We must come back to the idea of a relevant database. What concerns me is that if I had sexually abused my *own* children and you were unable to convict me of that, you could drop down to proceedings under the balance of probability and do something with me. Yet if I were a Thomas Hamilton character and should run a jigsaw club in my house, and allegations of sexual abuse were made against me, yet no conviction followed, you have not got a second tier for me to drop to. You cannot look at me under disciplinary procedures because I am not accountable to anybody; neither can you deal with me under the balance of probability. Why, therefore, do we not introduce a concept of accountability for all people who work with children in work clubs, youth clubs or even from their own home? We need to look at the whole use of references, and to train the interviewers and those monitoring supervision. In England the *Warner Report* helped us, but as I go around the country training those involved in staff selection it is clear that there are still major loopholes and resource issues in implementing this report.

We need to know how most sexual offenders operate. Let us listen to a social worker who was abusing while working in residential care; I want you to hear him talk, because sex offenders have knowledge and information that is invaluable and important for us if we are going to develop safety within our residential establishments. What I want to demonstrate is how people who abuse control the environment they are working in; how they have to control other people, how they make other people secondary victims. All of those issues are part of what we must understand if we are going to protect children.

Wyre: *Being on a course where practitioners are coming in as experts in the field, talking about abuse, when you are sitting there as an abuser, were you still able to be congruent?*
Respondent: *I used to come away feeling quite proud of myself - that may seem quite nasty, dirty - but I would get away with it. I was actually getting away with offending against the children whom others were trying to help. Yet I was an offender, actually sitting in a room, talking to these people....*
Wyre: *.... conning the professionals...*
Respondent: *absolutely.*

This is not a staff selection course, but I want to end by illustrating what we mean by the 'arena of safety and the aware culture'. Most people who sexually abuse do not abduct. They, for example, have a group of children and target one of them. There is 'accidental' touching, innuendo, play fighting. If that child says nothing the offender can then move into the abuse phase and during this phase it is unlikely that a child will ever tell they are being abused. You probably will not hear about it until they are an adult, if at all. And those are only the ones we actually *hear* about, because the vast number of children who are abused in this context we never hear of at all. How then do we deal with this testing-out phase? How do we set up arenas of safety and make the community safe? When I get a professional come to me who has been accused of sexual abuse he or she will often deny that they are involved, so I say to them 'what is it about your attitude, beliefs and behaviour that led to your being accused?' We took that strategy into the arena of organisations and institutions and we looked at their attitudes, beliefs and behaviour. We might find sexism, racism, inappropriate boundaries between professional and personal lives. We might find a whole range of worries and concerns giving more weight to the allegations being made.

I believe we need a thorough review and we do not need the piecemeal, knee-jerk response that often comes through media interest in a certain incident. We need to tackle this on many levels if we are ever going to protect the community. For me it is the only way forward. We must not think registration protects. It is simply a helpful tool as long as we take on board all the other issues that I have mentioned.

THE DIFFICULTIES ENCOUNTERED WHEN INVESTIGATING ABUSE THAT HAS TAKEN PLACE IN THE PAST

Terry Oates, Cheshire Constabulary

1 JOINT WORKING

While it is accepted that an inquiry of this kind is of an historical nature and as such does not fall within the parameters of the *Working Together* document under the *Children Act 1989,* nonetheless it was identified at an early stage that any such inquiry would require the cooperation of all agencies, especially the social services. It was because of this and their in-depth knowledge of the operations of children's homes that it was agreed to joint working. The responsibility for the investigation remained that of the police force, but it was recognised that appropriate consultation at both director and senior management levels was essential. It should be borne in mind that at the end of an inquiry of this nature our partners from the social services are likely to become embroiled in civil litigation which eventually could cost them, via the local authority, enormous sums of money. Early policy dictated that each force only had a responsibility to investigate those allegations which came within that force's boundaries, and that where allegations concerned children's homes in other force areas then that information should be passed to that host force for their consideration. There have been exceptions to this rule, where it has been found necessary to further the investigation against an individual offender by carrying out enquiries in other force areas, particularly where that individual has been employed, to ensure that all available evidence concerning that alleged offender is obtained. It is essential when contacting another force, concerning a complaint or allegation, that the initial formal contact should be made at assistant chief police officer (ACPO) level. Following liaison should then be maintained with a senior officer who can act as a collator for any subsequent complaints to ensure continuity. The difficulty encountered in this area was that complaints were forwarded to the respective divisions of the host force and as such, the enormity of the task, when so diluted, is not apparent. The decision to investigate any such allegations would remain at the discretion of the host force. An understandable reluctance to commit resources has been met on occasions. Clear guidelines have been drawn up outlining the roles and responsibilities of team members of both agencies. They are:

1.   This practice note is issued to confirm our previously-decided arrangements and to integrate further good practice in the light of the experience of the recent six week trial at Chester Crown Court. The focus of the guidance is the role of social services inquiry-linked liaison officers, although where necessary, reference is made to the associated role of involved police officers and their civilian witness

liaison assistant.

2.   The prime objective of all staff involved with the inquiry is to facilitate the bringing before the Courts of all available evidence relating to abuse allegedly committed against resident young people at the various establishments that are the subject of the inquiry. It is of crucial importance that individual complainants are supported through the processes of initial disclosure as well as in the subsequent periods whilst waiting for trial dates to be set, the immediate pretrial period, the processes at court and, lastly, the immediate and longer term period after court.

3.1 **Expected input in key stages**
Disclosure process Social services liaison officers will be available to advise and assist inquiry police officers and potential witnesses/complainants in successfully and sensitively achieving disclosure of material statements. Where potential witnesses or complainants do not initially or subsequently wish to make disclosures or statements, but where there is tangible need for the individual to receive further support or counselling, social services liaison officers will provide or facilitate that support on their own initiative in consultation with the senior investigating officer or his deputy. All potential witnesses seen in the course of the inquiry will be provided with the cards giving details of the independent National Society for the Prevention of Cruelty to Children (NSPCC) Helpline telephone number.

3.2   Although the *Memorandum of Good Practice Guidance* (joint video interviewing) and associated *Working Together* documents will normally not have direct application, given the current chronological ages of the potential witnesses we are dealing with in this inquiry, the guiding principles of these practice documents do have clear application for inter-agency roles and skills application within this inquiry. While the investigation is the primary role of the police, the skills of the social worker should be utilised to their best advantage, particularly when dealing with potential victims who may be reluctant to disclose.

3.3   **Support prior to trial date**
In accordance with Executive Policy No 22, *An Individual Victim When Identified,* the case officer will formulate a folder containing victim's details, the officer's assessment and full records of contact with victim. Contact to be made on a regular basis, unless request from a victim not to do so. Victims to be kept informed of case progress.
ii   This may be a period of many months. During this time, if any witness requires or requests counselling to deal with his reaction to making a disclosure statement, this will be facilitated (but not directly provided) through social services

liaison officers in consultation with the senior investigating officer or his deputy.

Involved social work staff already pro-actively linked to the inquiry will not at this stage, or any other pre-trial stage, directly provide counselling to any witness. This is straightforwardly to avoid any suggestion from defence counsel that witnesses may have been 'coached' by investigating teams in relation to their evidence.

3.4   Immediate pre-trial period

i   The respective roles of the linked police officer, social services liaison officers and the civilian witness support officer come into play especially in this period and through the actual trial. Great clarity and a real appreciation of the roles and responsibilities of each is required here.

ii   Fundamental police responsibilities at this time include: all arrangements for the confirmation of the location of the witness; notification to him of anticipated date he will be required at court; travel arrangements; production arrangements (if held at that time in custody); accommodation arrangements; related subsistence or practical matters; any special medical or quasi-medical needs that will have to be responded to; any essential financial reimbursements etc.

iii   At an appropriate time prior to the commencement of any trial, the police case officer must ensure that an introduction to the victim of the relevant social worker liaison officer is made. This will facilitate the requirements of victim/ witness care during the course of the trial and address any future victim care issues.

iv   Direct contact and support to victims during this period will only be made after full consultation with the senior investigating officer and his deputy. Details of all contacts made be entered onto victim log in accordance with Executive Policy No 22.

3.5 Through court

Under the direction of the senior police officer present and the involved police team officers, the police witness support assistant will retain knowledge of the presence, location and ordering of the witnesses as the prosecution is presented. Linked police officers present and social services liaison officers will work closely together with each other to provide a solid and corporate 'raft' of support to each witness at court. *By normal rules this will not include any witness' evidence with the witness prior to that being given in the court and the witness being discharged by the court.*

Wherever possible, social services liaison officers will be present in court when each complainant-witness is to give evidence. She/he will leave the court with the witness after evidence has been given and will then determine with the witness what immediate support or feedback they require or whether, at that stage, they wish simply to be left alone/go home/go off and talk later etc. This immediate support after evidence-giving will be provided by either the social worker alone or conjointly with the linked police officer or solely by the linked police *officer according to which individual or combination of individuals the witness appears most comfortable with.* In any event, the linked social worker or police officer at court will ensure that each witness is given a card with **both** the police and the social worker contact telephone numbers for future use.

3.6 Post court support
It is the clear expectation of both the Cheshire Social Services Directorate and the Assistant Chief Constables of Cheshire and Merseyside that all witnesses (especially witnesses who are victims/complainants) will be provided with whatever post-court support and counselling they may require. The clear view is that a duty of care towards all such witnesses exists and should be fulfilled. Here there may be a combination of practical/logistical/resource issues as well as appraisal as to whom any particular witness relates to best. From a social service perspective, it will be expected that social services liaison officers will make direct contact with each complainant-witness within three weeks after the end of the trial. This will be with a view to attempting to deal with any further resolvable issues arising from the evidence giving/trial outcome and to discuss and facilitate (not to provide) any longer term advice, assistance or counselling related to the individual's experience of abuse and its disclosure etc. The senior investigating officer will write at the end of each trial to each victim (whether called, or used, or neither) to advise them of the trial outcome and to thank them for their assistance in that process.

II   COUNSELLING PROCESS AND VICTIM MANAGEMENT
This   can be sub-divided into a number of different areas, commencing with:

i   Victim identification
When an individual has been identified as a potential victim it is important to ensure that appropriate support for that individual is available - even when either that person makes no disclosure or discloses but declines to do so in the way of a formal statement. In Cheshire arrangements were made with the NSPCC, who were prepared to counsel any individual contacting them on the understanding of complete confidentiality. Pre-printed cards were handed to all former residents of children's homes visited by police officers.

ii   Where victims were identified and made disclosures a victim's file was prepared and regular contact made in order to ensure that the victim was kept informed of the progress of the investigation. This was felt essential in view of the number of reported suicides in similar inquiries. Social services were fully-involved in this process, particularly bearing in mind the aftercare needed following any trial. It is important to emphasis the word 'victim' as opposed to 'witness'. The trauma these individuals had suffered is difficult to describe on these pages, and so it was important to understand that after such a dormant period of time in their lives 'Pandora's Box' was being opened and we had to be prepared for what came out. Experience has shown that not all victims are prepared to disclose when first interviewed. It has been necessary on occasions to build up a relationship, based on trust, before a disclosure is obtained. This can require a number of visits.

iii   One issue which became apparent was the impracticality to the inquiry teams of maintaining contact with the victims, due to both the number of victims and the size of the inquiry. This was overcome by the appointment of a witness liaison officer, who made regular contact with the victims and ensured proper records were maintained of changes of address etc.

iv   In the process of victim management, particularly at times of trials, victims would often be required to travel considerable distances and due to the vagaries of the criminal justice system they would have to be accommodated for up to three days in an hotel. It was found to be beneficial if the victims brought with them their wives, fiancees, friends - someone whom they trusted and who would act as a 'crutch' at a most difficult time. While the Crown Prosecution Service (CPS) would pay for all reasonable expenses of the victim/witness they could not pay for the support person and the social services agreed to meet this cost.

v   While the police have an important role to play pre-trial, then the social services would have an even greater role post-trial, and it is essential that victims were properly introduced to their social worker liaison officer at an early stage so that the 'letting-go' by the police was not seen as 'letting down'.

vi   In a small number of cases, victims will, because of their reluctance to be involved with social services, not wish to see a social worker. This will cause undoubted problems, but other agencies such as probation or the NSPCC can be utilized to good effect.

III   SOCIAL SERVICE FILES AND PUBLIC INTEREST IMMUNITY ISSUES

After consultation with other forces it was decided that the police would not seek to obtain social service files in respect of the victims. The reasons for this were:

i   The issues of disclosure rules.

ii   The size and volume of these files would have required a vast number of officers fully engaged on reading the files for any relevant information.

iii   It was felt that the information these files contained was so minor as not to affect the outcome of any prosecution.

iv Advice from counsel was that producing victims who were willing to testify far outweighed any amount of extraneous paper. Again, on advice of counsel, a nine-point letter was devised which was forwarded to the appropriate referring authority of each victim. The legal officer for that authority would then search the file and answer appropriately. The questions were formulated in such a way as to satisfy both defence and prosecution, and the legal officer, being an officer of the court, was accepted as acting impartially. Public interest immunity issues have raged throughout the various trials and court days set aside to deal with these issues. The police have not been involved in these arguments, but have been involved in the delays these issues have caused.

IV   ASSISTANCE BY NORTH WALES POLICE AND OTHER FORCES

In commencing any inquiry of this nature, it was essential to draw on any previous experiences of other forces. Three such enquiries provided the backbone to our inquiry:

- Leicestershire Children's Home (Frank Beck)
- Castle Hill School, Shropshire.
- North Wales Child Abuse

North Wales police were finalising their inquiry as we began ours, so liaison at senior management level was made and best practice sought. In conjunction with this, both the Leicester Children's Home report and advice and a report published on the investigation into Castle Hill School in Shropshire all provided relevant information and good practice guide.

V   DISCIPLINE HEARINGS AND DISCLOSURE ISSUES

The findings of the Police Complaints Authority (PCA) following the inquiry into the Leicester Children's Home recommended that any causes for concern should be passed on. The *Children Act 1989* dealt with the 'paramouncy principle', in which the interests of the child came first. Where it became apparent that a person still engaged in the child care arena had had a complaint or allegation made against them, consultation with the relevant agency was carried out, which included a risk assessment meeting. Upon completion of the investigation into the alleged offender, the authority would be informed of the result. Where a decision to suspend, following risk assessment, was made, disciplinary hearings would not normally be considered until the completion of the criminal investigation. However, there are exceptions. In those instances, due to the sub judice rules, the information supplied by the police to any tribunal would be of a very limited nature. Where, following the investigation and other consultation with the CPS, it was decided that no further action could be taken, then the victim, alleged offender and the relevant authority were fully informed. The difficulty then for the police, if disciplinary hearings were considered, was the supplying of information in breach of confidentiality agreements. The resolve was for the police to forward a letter on behalf of that authority to the victim asking the victim to contact the authority direct, thus releasing the police from any such agreements.

VI   CIVIL   LITIGATIONS   and   CRIMINAL   INJURIES COMPENSATION AUTHORITY (CICA)

Policy was set at the beginning of the inquiry that no police officer would discuss issues of compensation either via the CICA or through civil litigation. If a victim raised this subject he/she would be advised to seek proper legal advice from a solicitor. The benefit of this was experienced time and again when during the course of trials a defence tactic was to claim that the victim was either claiming from the CICA or suing the local authority for neglect or both and that disclosure statements had only been made for financial reward. In some instances it was suggested that police officers had promoted such ideas to obtain disclosures. It was not a successful ploy, because it had not happened. In an early report it was identified that one of the biggest issues would be the seduction of the police into civil litigation. That has yet to be tested, but there is little doubt that following the criminal trials the police will be subpoenaed to produce a vast amount of information concerning their investigations. Already a number of requests to attend CICA Boards have been received. Early liaison with the CICA was made to ensure their awareness of our investigation and the inevitable consequences. This has proved to be of value in streamlining communications and ensuring continuity. In respect of civil litigation we have only supplied copies of victims' statements to that victim's solicitors under strict conditions as to how the statement can be used. We have given no undertakings to supply any further information to victims' solicitors other than when ordered to do so by a court.

VII   STAFF SELECTION AND ATTRIBUTES

Where the vast majority of victims have over the passage of time become a part of the criminal fraternity then, when selecting officers to conduct this type of inquiry, it was important that they had a fair degree of experience. It was not necessary that they were detectives, albeit the vast majority were, but that the officer selected had investigative skills. Child protection officers certainly came into this category. A male victim is just as likely to disclose to a female officer as to her male colleague and there have been some instances where victims have made their preferences known. As a consequence it is felt that any inquiry team should be composed of mixed gender staff. It was also essential that all officers who interviewed alleged offenders had undergone the 'interview training skills course', as a defence tactic again was to challenge the competency of the interviewing officer.

Although in the main the investigation was one of an historic nature, in one instance the person under investigation was currently active in the child care arena.. Some officers were required who had 'joint interview skills' and had been trained jointly with social services for the purpose of joint video interviewing of potential victims. Clearly the inquiry could be of a protracted nature and not every officer is adept at staying with one inquiry for such a lengthy period of time. From a management point of view it was important to identify these individuals and ensure that they 'moved on' at the appropriate time. Other officers have the capacity to remain on such an inquiry without losing their enthusiasm and their experience is then essential to maintain the progress of the inquiry.

Welfare and morale have been raised as issues at strategy meetings. General counselling and an early identification of potential problems are essential and is a continuous process. The creation of a good team spirit is vital. The continued success of the inquiry has ensured a high level of morale. The subject of welfare is no different than for any other department and any problems in this area would be dealt with on their own merits.

The structure of the staff has evolved thus in the Cheshire inquiry:

- senior investigating officer
- deputy/administrator
- detective sergeants/team leaders
- dedicated disclosure officer
- dedicated tracing officer
- dedicated witness/victim liaison officer
- outside inquiry officers (investigators)
- HOLMES room personnel
- word processors
- dedicated social workers

The tracing officer is a detective constable who has been responsible for making contact with a large number of agencies to facilitate the tracing of former pupils and staff. His role has been essential in ensuring the continued progress of the inquiry teams in enabling them to obtain valuable evidence. The difficulties identified in some sixteen/twenty officers all arriving at the same agency to ascertain information were realized and so the tracing officer undertook this function, which has proven both efficient and cost-effective. It cannot be over-emphasised the need to fully brief all staff on the issues of sensitivity, confidentiality, victim-handling and the inevitable issues likely to be raised at subsequent trials. This awareness training must be carried out prior to the commencement of any investigation.

VIII   THE ROLE OF THE PRISON SERVICE

In the early stages of the inquiry difficulties were encountered in obtaining disclosures from inmates of prisons. This was due to the lack of privacy between the prisoner and the interviewing officer. After consultation with the Home Office Prison Liaison Section, it was accepted that where it was necessary to interview an individual who was either likely to disclose or believed to have been a victim, then arrangements were made for that person to be taken to a designated police station, the prisoner being given a 'cover story' prior to their return to prison. Victim support in these circumstances proved extremely difficult. However a network of prison/police liaison officers was contacted and, together with prison doctors and prison psychiatrists, these problems were overcome.

The next difficulty was encountered in the attendance of inmates at court for them to give formal evidence. Again these people would be reluctant to disclose in open court such horrific episodes, including buggery, when there was a possibility of their gaolers repeating these events back at the prisons from whence they came. The easy resolve to this was that Group 4 were contracted for all prisoner security at Crown Court, and it was made clear that any prisoner's evidence should not be repeated elsewhere. Following five trials it has been pleasing to note that there have been no known breaches of confidentiality. It is fair to say that good working relations were quickly established with Group 4, which resulted in a good deal of support while these victims were in the confines of court cells.

IX   INTERIM SEMINARS

In Cheshire two such seminars have been held, the first of which was subject of evaluation. There is no doubt that these seminars are extremely important in both a learning (training) sense and also as a vehicle for the passage of information. They also serve to engender a good team spirit and thus address the morale and welfare of the staff. The first seminar, held in October 1995, had two guest speakers who had been engaged on the Castle Hill School Inquiry in Shropshire. Their input was well-received, the only slight criticism being that it would have been even more beneficial to have heard these individuals at the beginning of the inquiry. The second seminar in 1996 was basically to ascertain whether or not expert evidence could be utilised at the forthcoming trials. Ray Wyre, a leading expert in the field of paedophiles, was invited to lecture to a selected audience of police, social workers and CPS lawyers. While it became apparent that the use of expert testimony would not be effective in a court room scenario, nonetheless the information gained provided good ammunition for cross-examination. Again, an earlier contact with this type of expert would have been beneficial in understanding the profile of offenders.

X   LOCATION OF THE MAJOR INCIDENT ROOM

Under normal circumstances even the concept of a major incident room outside a police station would not have been considered, however enquiries of this nature are, fortunately, not normal. While the police station provides the natural infrastructure, Home Office Large Major Inquiry (HOLMES) terminals, PNC bureau, criminal intelligence facilities and above all security, it is not necessarily the most ideal location. Because of the protracted nature of the inquiry, the inquiry itself is seen as a burden on resources. The officers who are then delegated the responsibility of conducting the inquiry are seen in a different light. Indeed the Cheshire officers were subject to a degree of isolation, such was their divorce from normal policing. That perhaps is indicative of canteen culture, but made a serious point in that support for such an enterprise must come from the top and be total and unanimous. Any joint inquiry must also take into consideration the views of the partnership. Police officers are comfortable working within a police station, but are social workers equally at ease? The ideal would of course be neutral ground where both sides could create their new 'home' and feel equally at ease. The reality of course is the financial burden this would create, especially in times of great frugality.

XI   COSTING AND BUDGET

From the outset, meticulous records have been kept to identify additional costs. There is an argument which suggests that the true figure for this inquiry should include the 'on cost'. Following a period of assessment a figure was agreed between the senior investigating officer and the force contingency fund holder. This figure was agreed to meet all additional costs of the inquiry, which included such areas as overtime, subsistence, fuel, mileage, accommodation, refreshments, stationery, and all other plethora of costs. Without doubt, at the time of trials, costs increase as the logistics of ensuring victims' attendance at the Crown Court requires a major input from the inquiry teams. Police officers and social workers act as 'minders' to these victims, a cost which cannot be passed to the CPS. Without this type of victim management it is doubtful whether all the victims would attend and give evidence.

Disclosure creates its own problems, not least in the actual reproduction of paper and costs of photocopying, which make quite large inroads into any budget. At the beginning of the Cheshire inquiry an inspector was appointed as the administrator for the inquiry. When that inspector retired, his role was widened and an inspector appointed who now operates as the deputy senior investigating officer/administrator. It must be accepted that this type of investigation cannot be considered as a local inquiry. The need to send the inquiry teams the length and breadth of the country is inevitable, with its inherent cost implications. An early policy decision ensured that geographical considerations were given in order to group enquiries together for both effectiveness and efficiency.

XII   SECURITY OF FILES

As already discussed, by virtue of the inquiry being based at a major police station the question of security does not feature greatly. However, the room in which HOLMES is contained and all relevant documentation is securely locked to ensure confidentiality.

XIII   MEDIA

A recognition that the correct use of the media, rather than a traditional 'no comment' answer, could prove of benefit. Early policy was established which dictated that the police press office acted as a conduit through which all press releases would pass. This was to ensure that the same messages were promulgated and that the media would not be able to 'play' quotes from one agency against another. This was accepted by all agencies. It was acknowledged that an investigation of this nature and size would engender massive media interest, and if it were not controlled, then adverse publicity could affect the ability of juries to deliberate impartially, and thus open up an avenue for defence. Following the first conviction of Alan Langshaw, in November 1994, the BBC (North West) published a half hour documentary titled *The Betrayed.* This was an extremely good and factual programme which dealt with the conviction and sentence (10 years) of Langshaw and did not incur into other investigations which were ongoing. Because of this programme other victims came forward, which greatly assisted the inquiry, and it was perceived that appropriate media coverage could be beneficial. BBC (Panorama) then made approaches to 'come on board', with the undertaking that nothing would be published until the conclusion of the full investigation. This was accepted and various filming has taken place to assist in the making of a future Panorama documentary. To date this has not presented any problems. In order to ensure no undue publicity prior to each trial, orders from the trial judge have been sought by the prosecution under the authority of *Section 11, Contempt of Court Act* 1981, which greatly restricts that which the media can publish. There are occasions where the victims and witnesses should be made aware of the media interests and advised accordingly.

XIV   STRATEGIC MEETINGS

Directors' strategy meetings have taken place approximately every six months, when following updates from the senior investigating officers (SIO) the strategy for the inquiry has been reviewed and if needed amended. This in no way has impinged on the actual investigation, but has sought to ensure that all the relevant agencies have the opportunity to voice any concerns over issues affecting their own organization. Regular weekly meetings between the SIO and the inquiry officers have proven value to disseminate information and ensure good working practice in prioritising the direction of the inquiry. Briefings prior to trials have proved essential. Operational orders previously prepared relating to the conduct of the trial and highlighting the roles and responsibilities of each team member have ensured a thoroughly professional approach. The same principle has been applied during the course of arrests of alleged offenders and their subsequent interviews.

XV   DEFENCE TACTICS
i   CICB
It has been essential to provide the courts in all trials with a list of those victims who have made a claim for criminal injuries compensation. While the defence invariably use this information in the hope of discrediting the witness, ie, 'you have made these allegations in order to claim money', the reality is that to date only 97 victims have sought compensation out of a total of over 300 victims; less than one- third.

ii   Civil claims
Again, when victims have been required to give evidence in cross-examination they have been asked if they are seeking compensation through the civil courts. From our own records, to date we have received requests for victims' statements from 108 solicitors, approximately one-third of all victims. The reality in both CICA and civil claims is that two-thirds of victims to date have not made any form of claim, which negates the defence tactic that those people making allegations are only doing so for financial gain. In dealing with this, the Crown has repeatedly said, 'yes this individual is making a claim; so what, he was abused, he is entitled, it is his right'. From the beginning of the inquiry all police officers were instructed not to discuss any form of compensation with victims, but if the subject was raised, to direct that individual to seek separate legal advice. This has proven to be beneficial as again the defence has sought to imply that officers obtaining disclosure statements have used the possibility of compensation as an inducement for obtaining that statement. Because of the initial policy, this was then easy to refute.

iii   Collusion by victims
In all trials there has been more than a mere suggestion that there is some form of conspiracy between the victims. Again this has been easily answered, not only because of the passage of time between the alleged offences and disclosure, but also the geographical location of many of the victims. A useful exercise was through the Prison Service identifying dates and locations when victims had been through the penal system. A chart could then be prepared showing that victims had not been incarcerated together, and thus were not in a position to form any conspiracy. A paragraph in the victim's statement relating to contact with former ex-residents also anticipated this line of attack.

iv   **Collusion by police and social workers**
This has not been raised as an issue in Cheshire.

v   **Character of victims**
The vast majority of victims have criminal records and as such are not seen in normal circumstances as ideal witnesses. It was important from the beginning for the investigation team to view these individuals as victims not as criminals. If we could come to terms with this, then it would be easier for that message to be portrayed to the courts. The defence in all trials have made great play of the victims' criminal records, i.e. 'how could these people be believed?'. In a number of instances victims, at the time they were abused, did not have criminal records and it could be argued only joined the criminal fraternity due to the abuse they suffered. The success of the inquiry to date proves the acceptance of the victims' allegations despite their criminal history.

vi   **Lack of medical or corroborative evidence**
This has not proved to be a particular issue. A statement from a medical expert in child abuse cases was obtained which clearly states that after such a passage of time there would be no medical evidence. This has been accepted by the defence, albeit previous medical records of the victims have been requested by the defence in an effort to contest buggery allegations. An examination of these records are worthy of consideration. In respect of corroboration the prosecution has sought to rely on the number of victims, each complaint corroborating another. The defence have had difficulty in addressing this issue, other than to say it is not true.

vii   **Consent of victim**
An issue raised by defence was that victims quite often admitted that they consented to the alleged abuse, but this was negated by the fact that they didn't have any options.

viii   **Encouragement by the media**
Has not been an issue in any of the trials to date.

XVI   ROLE OF THE EXPERT WITNESS

The expert witness has already been mentioned at paragraph 9 and 15(f). It is fair to say that our own expertise has developed as the inquiry progressed, our own understanding of 'grooming' techniques has improved as disclosure statements have been obtained. As mentioned at paragraph 9, input at an earlier stage from a leading expert in paedophiles would have been of greater benefit in our own education. There are a number of reasons why victims have not previously disclosed, including fear, shame, guilt etc. Early awareness of these matters by the inquiry officers assists when interviewing victims and is more likely to lead to a fuller disclosure of information.

XVII NETWORKING ISSUES

The terms 'networking' or 'paedophile ring' are synonymous and at all times the investigation has sought to establish whether such 'networking' or 'ring' exists. To ensure no evidence was overlooked, the HOLMES computer was utilized and to date no such evidence has been obtained. That is not to say that these things do not exist, as it is difficult to accept that paedophiles working in the same or similar children's homes are not aware of each other's activities. Many of these offenders are territorial; having spent time, effort and money grooming children for abuse they are not then likely to pass them to another for abuse. Links between offenders can and have been established; the fact the offenders operate in the same premises and at the same time are known. Other links can be introduced such as different offenders from different establishments being known to each other. However, hard evidential fact as to 'networking' or 'paedophile rings' has not been established, leaving only speculation.

XVIII REVIEW PROCESS
While there was no precedent for an external review, i.e. the offences were detected, it was useful to have an overview of an independent source, and confirmation that the inquiry was proceeding on the right lines. An inquiry of this nature is not above scrutiny and provided it is thoroughly investigating all complaints, cannot fear such examination. Indeed, at the end of this inquiry there is little doubt that we shall become subject of either a judicial review or public inquiry and so checks and balances help to ensure good working practices.

XIX THE ROLE OF CPS AND SPECIAL CASE WORKERS
Early in this inquiry the police requested the facility of a special case prosecutor. Unfortunately this was not made available, primarily due to financial constraints within the CPS. This has presented difficulties in that the police have always been expected to work to a time scale, but the Crown appear not to have been under the same constraints. Vital information concerning dates of hearings have not always been passed to the police and opportunities lost to address contentious issues raised by defence. On two occasions the defence has been successful in having the indictment severed, which has meant that not all the evidence is heard before one jury, thus weakening the case. This occurs where an offender is arrested, charged and indicted and further evidence is then obtained of additional abuse. The additional evidence is then subject of an application for a voluntary bill of indictment and placed before a High Court judge. Once granted, the trial judge is then asked to enjoin the two indictments and the offender stands trial on all matters. The defence successfully claimed that the application for the voluntary bill was too late in the proceedings and as such afforded the defence no time for discovery. The prosecution then attempted to introduce the additional evidence as similar fact and, while it was accepted as such, it was not allowed again because of the lateness of the application. At no stage was it suggested that this problem was created by the police in the late submission of papers, but proved the necessity

of having a special case prosecutor with sole responsibility for this one inquiry.

In total, 96 persons have had allegations made against them, 70 of which have been processed and 15 being the subject of prosecution. Of the 55 not being prosecuted, the decision to take no further action is now being reviewed by counsel to ensure continuity and appropriate decision making. The volume of work involved in this would certainly have preoccupied a special case prosecutor full-time and benefited the inquiry. Meetings with counsel prior to trials have proved of immense benefit to both parties and ensured the smooth progress of subsequent trials. In the first instance the investigation was conducted using the 'mushroom system' whereby as an individual disclosed abuse, he would name other persons he believed it would be of benefit to interview. Initial parameters were agreed in context of how far back the investigation should go. The children's homes had all been closed, so one end of the parameter was easy to determine. The other end was determined by virtue of the commencement of employment of the individual complained against, with an override of 20 years, which it was argued beyond that time would open up the avenue for defence to claim 'abuse of process'. In reality the investigation has had to delve back even further due to the nature of allegations received and the fact that some of those alleged against are still working in the child care arena. In the process of going back such a period of time, it was agreed as a principle to 'dip sample' approximately 20% of former pupils before 1974. If any disclosures were forthcoming, further 'dip sampling' at a rate of 10% would be conducted until such time as no disclosures were made. At the same time and depending on the information received, we have always retained the flexibility to fully investigate any period where it was felt either appropriate or necessary. This was highlighted in the case of an offender who had been working in Cheshire between 1966-69. The 'dip sampling' revealed horrific allegations and this individual was discovered to be working in Cambridge at a senior level in social Services. Because of these facts a full investigation was then undertaken by both Cheshire and Cambridge Police. He now stands indicted on some 47 counts, primarily of buggery, with 40 victims.

Other procedures undertaken in order to trace potential victims included the sending of a registered letter to the homes of former residents of the establishments under investigation. This had the following effects:

• it enabled us to confirm contact with former residents, ie the signing for the registered letter;
• it made that individual aware that an investigation was taking place;
• it provided an opportunity for potential victims/witnesses to contact the inquiry;
• although undertaken on a limited scale, and not recommended as a primary

line of inquiry, it has proved to be cost-effective. This places an onus on the individual to come forward and disclose where appropriate.

XXI   HOME OFFICE LARGE MAJOR INQUIRY (HOLMES) and I.T

In simple terms it would not have been effective to conduct this inquiry without the use of the Home Office Large Major Inquiry System (HOLMES) computer. While there are guidelines and conventions governing the staffing of any HOLMES room, as with all systems it has been used to benefit the inquiry and not 'run it'. Staff therefore within the room have been multifunctional and not dedicated to one specific task due to resource implications. The criteria for this has been that the offences alleged are primarily detected. Clearly there is now a wealth of information stored within HOLMES. The question to be asked is what happens to all this information when the inquiry is concluded. The National Criminal Intelligence Service (NCIS) has been consulted and are interested in obtaining copies of computer tapes to update their own records. Other technology essential to the inquiry has included the appropriate use of voice mail boxes, giving out information to potential victims/witnesses at times when the incident rooms have not been staffed.

XXII PRO-ACTIVE APPROACH TO PAEDOPHILE ACTIVITIES

In any system there are those who will seek to abuse that system for their own benefit. Paedophiles have clearly abused the child care system in that they have used it throughout the 1960s, 70s and 80s for their own perversion. There is too much evidence nationally to ignore the above facts and if as a society we are serious in our attempts to root out these purveyors of evil, who have corrupted generations of children who have passed through the care system, then we must do so in a pro-active manner. The evidence of this inquiry showing wholesale abuse is testimony to the fact that abused children who become adults do not (in the main) come forward and volunteer information. They feel too ashamed of what they believe they have allowed to happen to them. The culture of the paedophile is the transference of guilt and they are extremely successful in doing so, hence the lack of complaints. Only by re-visiting these centres of abuse and establishing contact with those who were abused can we hope to discover the true scope of abuse and deal with it appropriately. Today's climate has never been more conducive to the undertaking of this kind of inquiry, but to do so takes commitment from all concerned. Only then can we say that the future generations of our children likely to pass through the care system are free from abuse.

Another issue is that of the single allegation which is uncorroborated. It is inevitable that this allegation will fail to lead to any prosecution. However, it is essential that it is fully recorded and documented so as to ensure that if at any stage in the future the same individual becomes the subject of another allegation the first matter can be clearly referred to and be available. Consideration should also be given to any future complaints which relate to those matters which have been finalized and dealt with through the courts. Force policy will have to dictate the introduction of a system that will be capable of addressing and dealing appropriately with any subsequent complaints of this nature.

XXIII DISCLOSURE

With such a complex inquiry, the appointment of an officer capable of dealing with disclosure is essential. This officer must have the ability to read and assimilate vast amounts of documentation and make reasoned decisions concerning sensitive and non-sensitive issues. The role of the disclosure officer is less demanding at the beginning of the inquiry and can have a dual role such as research officer. Following the arrest and charging of an offender, this officer's role intensifies and he must have a HOLMES viewing facility. HOLMES in itself is not the ideal vehicle for disclosure material, but it is understood that 'bolt on' packages are available, at a price. With nearly 7,000 nominals, 4,500 actions and 2,500 statements, it is hardly surprising that it has become a dedicated task. The need for close liaison with the CPS in relation to disclosure issues is paramount.

XXIV OFFENDERS

One of the difficulties encountered in this inquiry was the timing of the arrest of alleged offenders. The first criteria faced was whether or not the individual concerned was still a practitioner in the child care arena. Where this was the case and multiple disclosures obtained, then an arrest was implemented whether or not the inquiry was completed, simply because the risk of allowing another child to be abused would leave the police open to serious criticism. Where only one or two allegations were received against an individual, then risk assessment meetings were held with the appropriate agency to determine whether there was a need for an immediate arrest, or allow the investigation to progress further. Difficult decisions had to be taken in respect of the above two categories of persons. In the last category, those who were no longer engaged in the child care arena posed no problems and so the investigation could run its course before decisions were made.

SOME THOUGHTS ARISING FROM
THE RECENT CONFERENCE

Tony Butler QPM, Chief Constable,
Gloucestershire Constabulary

- *Six more sex fiends go free - cops helpless*
- *Sex offenders to go free without controls*
- *A day in the life of a freed child sex killer*
- *Fears over unmonitored paedophiles*
- *Six evil predators bound for freedom*

These were just some of the headlines that appeared in the national press the day after the ISTD/Sussex Police conference. Members of the public reading the articles under these headlines could not be criticised for believing the seminar had come to the conclusion that there were no effective, practical measures in place or being considered, for dealing with sex offenders. Only a few weeks later we saw how powerful the media can be when the release of Sidney Cooke from Wandsworth Prison was reported. The effect of the media in that instance, building on the reporting of events such as the ISTD/Sussex Police conference, has left the statutory agencies and other bodies with an increasingly difficult task in providing assurance to the public that a lot of work is being carried out quietly and thoughtfully to try and ensure that greater protection is afforded to children and other vulnerable persons. Serious questions have to be asked as to whether, with hindsight, it was appropriate or wise to conduct a debate amongst professionals on such a complex and sensitive issue in front of the media, students and television programme makers. Their presence prevented informed debate and restricted delegates with expert knowledge from contributing positive messages to the seminar. There are many sensitive operational matters which cannot, for obvious reasons, be discussed in public. The debate therefore left many delegates shaking their heads in despair that they were being expected to tackle these issues without legislation, Government support, funding and inter-agency co-operation at a national level. Reading the newspaper headlines the next day must have fuelled those concerns. This response then is an attempt to redress the balance, to explain that, whilst no perfect guaranteed solutions exist, a lot is being done to improve the mechanisms for the assessment, release, monitoring and management of sex offenders in the community.

The *Sex Offenders Act 1997* placed the lead responsibility for the management of sex offenders with the police service and with it a clear expectation that forces, jointly with other agencies, would develop a risk assessment strategy. Many forces had already developed protocols between themselves, probation and social services to manage the risks posed by dangerous offenders but in discussions with the Home Office it was clear there was a need for further process which would manage convicted sex offenders, irrespective of whether they required to register or not.

As forces worked hard to develop sex offender risk assessment processes on a multi-agency basis it was obvious that it would be helpful to forces for there to be an accepted national model which could be adapted locally to fit individual needs. Such a model, as well as preventing division and misunderstanding, would allow for consistent decision making throughout the country. Under the direction of the Association of Chief Police Officers (ACPO) Crime Committee a small working party has been formed, with representatives drawn from the police and probation, to examine how best we can achieve sonic form of national guidance in risk assessment. We hope the working party will be able to make their initial findings available by mid summer 1998.

Introduction of the *Sex Offenders Act 1997* had significant operational implications for the police service. Early discussions provided a useful catalyst to review arrangements at a local and national level for the police response to sex offenders. In that context the Director General, National Criminal Intelligence Service (NCIS) agreed it was essential to bring into consideration the part NCIS, and in particular the NCIS Paedophile Unit played in this area of policing. It was readily acknowledged that police resources had to be tightly focused and organised in such a way that maximum benefit could be achieved. A small working group was established to review the current role of the unit in relation to sex offenders committing crimes against children and to consider how the police service, in collaboration with NCIS, could improve the effectiveness of current arrangements. Representatives from ACPO, the Association of Chief Police Officers [Scotland] (ACPOS), HM Customs and Excise, NCIS and the prison service, have joined the group. An interim report is expected shortly.

In early May 1998 the Home Office announced the formation of a new national steering group to look at the issue of high profile sex offenders and that announcement was welcomed by the ACPO Crime Committee and the Association of Chief Officers of Probation (ACOP). The announcement formalised arrangements to identify strategies for dealing with the release of high profile sex offenders. Two of the areas that will be looked at when a person is released are how to overcome the major difficulties about accommodation and the significant costs that can be incurred by the police and probation in re-housing that person. There has been a great willingness to house offenders in existing facilities but this has recently been difficult to achieve because of media reporting. Discussions at a national level between the Home Office, probation and police are a powerful partnership to solve problems incapable of resolution at a local level.

The Government has clearly stated that it regards the protection of children as one of its highest priorities and that it is committed to ensuring there are measures in place to prevent children being sexually abused or exploited. *The Sex Offenders Act 1997* has introduced registration requirements for sex offenders and allowed for extra-territorial jurisdiction to deal with those persons committing offences abroad. It is intended that later this year the Home Office will commence work to evaluate how effective the legislation and guidance has been and the Home Office has indicated a willingness to consider refinement of the legislation if the research identifies a need. Sex Offender Orders will be introduced as part of the *Crime and Disorder Bill*. This will allow the police to apply to a civil court to direct the behaviour of a person previously convicted of a relevant sex offence. Breach of one of these orders carries a substantial penalty. Following on from a Memorandum of Understanding signed by the UK and the Philippines in August 1997, a joint initiative - ASEM 2 (Asia and European Meeting) conference, is being organised to consider how to combat the sexual exploitation of children and sex tourism. Research is being funded and undertaken in the United Kingdom, Europe and throughout the world so that we gain a better understanding of the issues and how to respond to them.

In a relatively short article it has not been possible to cover all of the measures and aspects of work that are on going in this complex area of policing. What I hope this article will achieve is to persuade professionals who are working with sex offenders that they are not working alone. No-one under estimates the challenges but we have made significant progress in the past two/three years and there is commitment and willingness to work together.

In ending, let me return to the beginning of this article. Sensational newspaper headlines sell newspapers, but they tend to achieve nothing else. We need to have rational, balanced debate involving informed and professional people. That debate, if it is to be successful, must take place out of the glare of the media. A measure of our success in tackling these difficult issues in a thoughtful way might be the absence of sex offender banner headlines in the future.

NEVER MIND THE FACTS, WHERE'S THE STORY?

Gill Mackenzie, Chief Probation Officer, Gloucestershire Probation Service

Has the recent extraordinary level of public reaction to the cases of Cooke, Oliver and other sex offenders safeguarded children and promoted public protection? How competent are the authorities at dealing with the demons of the late nineties? In the midst of the media furore and public protests outside police stations in Bristol and Somerset, two events occurred that can assist in answering those questions. In April 1998 the Association of Chief Officers of Probation conducted a survey of probation services in England and Wales to ascertain the impact of public over-reaction to sex offenders and at the end of the same month Her Majesty's Inspectorate of Probation published its report *Exercising Constant Vigilance: The Role of the Probation Service in Protecting the Public from Sex Offenders*. Both events were well covered by the media in terms of the headline findings, but this article provides an opportunity to describe them in greater detail.

The findings of the survey highlight three areas of particular concern: the role of the media; attacks on innocent adults and children; and the plight of targeted sex offenders away from the supervision and surveillance of the probation and police services. Ten examples of the disturbing consequences of press publicity have been forwarded to the Press Complaints Commission. These included instances such as the local paper which published not only the court case, but the address and a photograph of the block of flats where the offender lived. A resident of the flats, mistaken for the offender, was beaten so severely that the attacker was charged with attempted murder. Another local paper that kept its own register provoked numerous incidents, the most severe of which was the burning of an offender's home, where he lived with his wife and child. The paper also printed the child's name. Innocent adults have been subject to assaults and fly-posting campaigns. Relatives of sex offenders have been abused and pilloried. In a particularly sad case, the elderly sister of a sex offender was subjected to a continuous campaign of harassment occasioning the involvement and great concern of Victim Support.

Also worrying are the times when good systems of supervision and monitoring have been wrecked. There were several such examples in the survey. One offender, no longer on licence but still being monitored by the probation and police services, disappeared from contact after his photograph was displayed on lamp posts. In another case a man considered to be a risk, but in voluntary contact with the probation service and under close surveillance by the police, was exposed by a tabloid newspaper. Following his second change of address he became untraceable.

How do we as a society find the middle path between non-protective indifference and the counter-productive public hostility described in the survey, whereby we can calmly take sensible steps to protect children? Using the analogy of Aids, we have to move away from the frenzied and hopeless quest that was such a characteristic of the early 80's (to identify every HIV carrier in order to corral 'them' and hence contain the risk) to the much more effective, uniformly protective and educated stance that currently operates (your dentist does not demand to know whether you are HIV positive, rather he/she wears rubber gloves). Perhaps in a similar way, with a greater knowledge generally available in the community about what constitute the most likely risks of abuse to children and how these risks can be lessened, we might begin to respond rationally to the problem. Much of this information already exists and in easily understandable language; the NSPCC publish an excellent booklet for parents and carers. Perhaps the next media campaign should be an educative one.

The report of the Probation Inspectorate on how the probation service carries out its duties in relation to sex offenders clearly acknowledges that it is 'a time of unprecedented public debate and concern' on this issue. It is also able to point to the very positive way in which the probation service has responded to the challenge of working with this high profile category of offender.

Amongst the aspects of the service's work enumerated as commendable were:

- protection of the public was unambiguously identified as its central purpose;
- recognition of the distress and harm experienced by victims was its primary focus;
- a high level of vigilance was being exercised;
- the rigour of supervision was evident;
- collaborative work between agencies was extensive and increasing.

The report describes in detail its findings in all areas of work with sex offenders, from the policy, planning and organisational framework to the nature and purpose of the interventions. It notes the expansion over recent years of group work programmes which are structured on the evidence of research findings and recommends that this approach and its associated expertise is used more systematically in individual supervision. However, not all offenders given a community sentence received an order requiring them to consider the seriousness of their behaviour. Inspectors were surprised to discover that in a substantial minority of cases (548 at the end of 1996) courts were imposing Community Sentence orders on sex offenders. Although satisfied that staff were ensuring that safe, sensible working arrangements were provided, the report clearly indicates that the probation service and, by inference, sentencers, should be especially cautious before imposing such a sentence.

A sophisticated, well-organised group work programme for sex offenders is reflected in the report's findings that only one third of through-cases reviewed by Inspectors had attended the programme. Consequently, one of the ten recommendations focuses on the need for the Home Office, Prison Department and the probation service to 'devise a comprehensive strategy to tackle offending for all those sex offenders sentenced to imprisonment'.

Of the other recommendations, perhaps the most important relates to adolescent sex offenders (aged between 13 and 17 years). Here the Inspectors had found 'the largest and most worrying gap in provision'. The report urges the Home Office and the Department of Health to collaborate in the development of systematic assessment, intervention and relapse prevention services, observing that without such provision, opportunities to intervene at an early stage before behaviour patterns had become entrenched, were lost.

It is a detailed and encouraging report bearing 'testimony to skilled and persistent work on the part of probation staff'. Whether it will inform the current debate is quite another matter.

THE DUTCH PERSPECTIVE

John Staps, Head of Youth and the Vice Squad, Rotterdam

Sexual abuse and public debate

Every few years the discussion about public ethics and decency and the role the authorities should play in this, flares up. In the late sixties public ethics changed drastically in the Netherlands and abroad; liberty and equality (liberalisation and democratisation) dominated public debate. The oppressive sexual ethics of the preceding years were undermined by the 'sexual revolution'. There were free sexual relations and the authorities were no longer in a censoring role. In the years following this period, a new trend emerged as a reaction to too much permissiveness; the protection of victims. Since then these two trends have been diametrically opposed, leading to the rights of the victims versus those of the perpetrators. Perpetrators and victims both organised lobby groups and fought for more rights and these lobby groups are closely involved in the drafting of bills.

It so happened that in a meeting about the drafting of new regulations concerning child pornography I found myself sitting opposite the president of a paedophile lobby group. In many countries the idea of an official group that stands up for the interests of paedophiles is unheard of, let alone the fact that their opinion about a new bill would be sought. Speaking as a police officer, I cannot always be proud of the situation in my country.

With the breaking of the taboo regarding sexual behaviour and particularly that of criminal sexual behaviour, media attention increased enormously. Apart from the positive effect of this attention, such as the fact that victims became more outspoken, there are also the negative effects of media witch hunts. Lawyers claim that because of the media coverage, their client is labelled (convicted) from the beginning and a fair trial is no longer possible. Judges sometimes share this opinion and take it into account when determining the sentence. For the victim the media attention may result in attendant victimisation: children who are pointed at at school or are being pestered so much that they have to move.

Marc Dutroux, the defendant in the Belgian sex abuse scandal, added fuel to the flames and unwittingly made the organising of an international conference on this subject, such as the one held in Stockholm in August 1996, more important than ever. Never has sexual abuse been so much in the picture and never before has society as a whole been so preoccupied with it. All of a sudden everyone knows how to deal with the problem. Sometimes people are considerate, understanding and sensible, but often they are rash and extremely emotional What people suggest should be done, varies roughly from the death penalty or compulsory castration of the perpetrator, to therapy and rehabilitation.

Practical examples of a return into society: setting the scene
It is not only in the United Kingdom that there has been a discussion about whether society has the right to trace convicted sexual offenders who have been punished and/or sexual offenders who have completed treatment and then to make their identities and backgrounds public. In a village in the Netherlands this year, a twenty-one year old man was about to return to the village after a period spent in detention under a hospital order, which ended on his twenty-first birthday, in accordance with the statutory provisions. In 1994 this retarded boy had been convicted for the sexual abuse of 24 children. The therapists who treated him were of the opinion that he had not yet been cured, but there was no legal ground to keep him any longer in detention under a hospital order. The boy chose to return to his own village and live with his parents. The inhabitants of the village took civil legal action against him and his parents to force them to move. The judge, however, placed the problem back into the hands of the local authorities.

In Canada there is Bobby Oatway. This man was sentenced to thirteen years in prison for raping his own children and his sister-in-law. His victims swore they would pursue him till he died and would continue to make his identity and his acts public. After having been in prison for ten years, a period during which Bobby underwent intensive therapy, he was secretly transferred to an institute run by an aftercare and resettlement organisation, at the other end of the country. There, for a period of three years, he was to be prepared to return to society. The behavioural therapists estimated that the chance of relapse was very small. He was traced, however, and the inhabitants of Toronto turned against him and, later, also against the other inmates of the institute. Despite the fact that in the ten years the institution had been there not one of the convicted offenders had been arrested for a new offence, the inmates were described as 'walking time bombs'. The local community tried to have the institution closed. Despite continuing protests, night and day, the community eventually agreed to Oatway having walks under permanent supervision and gradually the protests decreased. But Bobby Oatway's victims started to put up posters with photographs all over town and a new series of protest demonstrations began. During an election campaign, these protest demonstrations were backed by local politicians. Bobby Oatway could not stand it anymore; even in his room he had to listen to threats against him as a megaphone was being used. His fellow inmates also turned against him. In a prison in another part of Canada, dozens of offenders in a wing for sexual offenders suffered grievous bodily harm during a riot. Oatway was in a dilemma; he could return to prison for three years or continue the present situation.

I will return to these cases at the end of this paper.

The nature and extent of criminal sexual behaviour in the Netherlands

To clarify the present situation in the Netherlands concerning criminal sexual behaviour, the following figures are necessary:

Sexual abuse of women

According to the statistics, annually 120,000 women in the Netherlands are confronted with some form of undesired sexual contact. 26,000 stated they had experienced sexual assault or rape and the other women talked about sexual intimidation, which, legally speaking, is seen as a 'minor offence' and is not thought to be punishable. Only 14% of these 26,000 sexual assaults and rapes are reported to the police each year. The dark number - the number of cases that have not been reported to the police - is substantial.

Sexual abuse of children

In the first half of the nineties, annually 1,650 cases of sexual abuse of children came to the notice of the police. It is highly probable that here, too, the dark number is substantial. Several Dutch and foreign surveys demonstrate that 2 - 7% of all boys and 15 - 34% of all girls have experienced some form of sexual abuse before they are eighteen.

What *is* known is that the majority (according to the statistics, approximately 90%) of the offences are committed by people who are close to the victim; one of the parents, for example, or an uncle, a family friend, a teacher or a sports coach.

It is very important to have a good understanding of the backgrounds and motives of perpetrators and their relation with their victims. One the one hand this is necessary for the determination of the sentence and the nature and duration of (compulsory) therapy. On the other hand this may help with regard to preventive measures, such as taking action when the potential perpetrator is still young. After ten years of experience in this field, there is now quite some expertise in the Netherlands.

Punishment and treatment in the Netherlands and the risk of relapse

All perpetrators of sexual offences have, as a central element in the development of sexual aggression, inadequate attachment in their families and resulting inadequate social competence. Often there are also other fundamental, stressful events during the period the offence is committed.

Various factors play a role in the determination of punishments and measures. The personality characteristics of the perpetrator; the violence he used; previous convictions for violent offences. The Public Prosecutions Department will ask a behavioural therapist for advice about the risks of relapse. Perpetrators who satisfy a number of conditions can be treated in an ambulatory setting. However, to qualify for ambulatory treatment the offender should not have used extreme violence. A perpetrator who has used extreme violence can be made to spend time in a special clinic; the time spent there can be extended every two years, following a risk assessment.

If one looks at the treatment objectives, it is clear that treatment definitely does not mean the perpetrator is treated gently. However, it has been shown that treatment is more effective than imprisonment. There should be a good relationship between the offence committed and the punishment and treatment. This relationship has to be determined individually.

The risks of relapse

Table 1

Risks of relapse (after five years and longer) taken from an average of 27 surveys of sexual offenders	
Exhibitionists	33%
Rapists	23%
Paedosexuals (aimed at boys outside the family)	35%
Paedosexuals (aimed at girls outside the family)	18%
Paedosexuals (aimed at children within the family)	9%

Source: *Hall 1990, Mc Grath 1991, Prentkey et al, 1997, Quinsey et al, 1995*

Table 2

Relapse risk factors for sexual offenders taken from an average of 27 surveys of sex offenders
• previous sexual offences • other types of deviant sexual behaviour, past and present • choice of a boy (rather than a girl) as their victim • previous non-sexual offences • anti-social personality disorder (psychopathy/sociopathy) • use of expressive aggression • extent of sexual preoccupation with children • choice of an unknown person as their victim • the sexual extent of the offence (penetration versus caresses) • being under thirty • alcohol abuse • impulsiveness in style of living • no supportive, social network • low social competence • mood disorders (chronically angry/afraid/depressed) • denial of previous sexual offences • trivialising of offence • no treatment • no supervision of after-care and resettlement organisation or withdrawal from this

Source: as previous

Influenced by promising treatment programmes and good relapse figures achieved by sexual offenders in the USA, Canada and in the Netherlands, elements of a cognitive therapy approach are being implemented. The prevention of relapse programme is aimed at self control rather than a cure. In Rotterdam there is successful training-of-sexual-offenders therapy. For a period of two years, during one hundred sessions, perpetrators have cognitive behavioural therapy in groups, which aims at self disclosure, impulse control and analysis of the offence scenario. If the perpetrator does not satisfy the conditions for attending therapy sessions, a term of imprisonment is hanging over his head. In addition to the therapy, difficult situations such as obtaining a job, a house, assistance in case of addiction are also worked on.

Whenever possible, the family and the victims are involved in the therapy, in order to be able to create sufficient factors for monitoring purposes. Each inclination to relapse then comes to the attention of the therapist. As far as we know, none of the persons involved has so far relapsed and many people in the Netherlands are monitoring the therapy closely. The problem is, however, that only 20% of the perpetrators are presently being treated. The institutions providing this type of therapy have a shortage of capable therapists and it is hoped that by demonstrating the success of the therapy, the number of therapists will be increased. Meanwhile, the therapists stress to politicians that treatment as a measure should be imposed more often.

Conclusions

As a society we should do all we can both to tackle sexual abuse and to prevent it. Internationally and nationally, people work hard to analyse the bottlenecks in the approach to and the prevention of sexual abuse so as to eliminate them. Uniform legislation is one of way forward. Society should gain more confidence in the system of punishment and other measures by being better informed of the nature and the results of treatment methods. Treatment is an effective measure of prevention as it is aimed both at the perpetrator and the victim.

Under our constitution both perpetrators and victims in this liberal country of mine have rights which are often diametrically opposed. It is a case of the protection of society versus the protection of the privacy of a perpetrator and their right to a fair chance to make a new start. The chance of a return to society by a perpetrator who has been punished, fully treated, yet *still* demonstrates a substantial chance of relapse, is very small. At the moment police involvement is the exception. The judiciary, after-care and resettlement organisations and local police should together develop a monitoring system. The data in this system should not be made public, but should only be retrievable for the authorities concerned.

Making the backgrounds of perpetrators public is the wrong approach to the problem and I do not think anything is gained by this. Indeed, fear will become the public's strongest enemy. This can be an uncontrollable fear, for the behaviour of the public when informed of the perpetrator cannot be predicted - perhaps even less so than the behaviour of the perpetrator himself. Most perpetrators are co-operative during therapy and imprisonment, because there is an important reward; return to society. This motivates the offender to continue the therapy. Should this reward not be there, then they would have no reason to win back their self respect and attend therapy.

To return to the two cases I cited earlier. Eventually the boy was given compulsory treatment under another type of legislation. This means that the problem has been put off to the end of his treatment. But when he has completed treatment - and the risk of a relapse would be minimal, according to the experts - then it would be best if he went back to his own village, so that he could be monitored as closely as possible. However, for the victims and their families it is unacceptable for them to come across this boy in their local supermarket. Even though the boy might not commit any more sexual offences, there is a risk of relapse for the victims, because they may not be able to cope with their traumas anymore. For the victims it would be best if the boy moved to another town or village, without people in his new surroundings knowing his background and thus lessening the chance of his being hunted.

Bobby Oatway is a perpetrator whom behavioural experts thought presented a minimal risk of relapse if he were monitored regularly and Oatway agreed to this condition. However, because of what society did to him, his resentment has become so strong, that it increases the risk that he will now commit another violent offence. He is an outcast, both in and outside prison. He compares himself to an animal that is locked in a cage and is constantly being prodded. He has chosen to be transferred to a prison for the remainder of his detention (three years) instead of having monitored rehabilitation outside the prison system. Yet whichever way you look at it, in three years' time he will be released from his cage. His victims have sworn they will trace him again. In a country such as Canada - and this applies to other countries as well - it is possible to make a new start, without people knowing your background and with a new identity. If, in principle, compulsory monitoring by an after-care and resettlement organisation could be permanently imposed then I believe that Bobby Oatway deserves a new chance. The suspended part of his sentence could work as a sword of Damocles. Otherwise, there is only one alternative: lifelong imprisonment.

I think monitoring this small group of perpetrators undergoing rehabilitation is desirable, but they should be monitored by people who think sensibly and are not rash or driven by emotions. While we are busy watching the registered perpetrators, let us not forget that our children run a greater risk of being sexually abused by someone they know.

SPEAKERS DETAILS

Allan Bowman was appointed Director of Social Services for Brighton and Hove Council in 1996. Prior to this he was Director of Social Services for Fife Social Services. As a Director he has been very active in the field of child protection. He also has extensive experience of working with offenders and has close links with Apex Scotland and the Airbourne Initiative, which promotes alternatives to prison regimes. Allan Bowman is particularly interested in forging links with Europe and personally launched the *European Year of Older People* in the United Kingdom.

Penny Buller has been Chief Probation Officer for East Sussex since 1991 and is a current member of the Parole Board for England and Wales. Her career in the probation service has spanned 25 years. She worked in Bristol before moving to Oxfordshire, where she was appointed Assistant Chief Probation Officer. Penny Buller was seconded to HM Inspectorate of Probation for 18 months prior to taking up her present post.

Tony Butler became Chief Constable of Gloucestershire Constabulary in 1993. Previous to that he was Assistant Chief Constable (Support Services, then Operations) for the Leicestershire Constabulary, before becoming Deputy Chief Constable in 1990. Tony Butler joined Warwickshire Constabulary in 1964 and, following a period of secondment, gained a joint honours degree from Birmingham University, which was followed by a PhD based on extensive research into the psychological implications of policing. As a member of the Association of Chief Police Officer's Crime Committee he has had a lead responsibility for matters relating to juvenile crime, child protection and sex offenders. He is currently a member of the Government's Task Force on Youth Crime.

Nick Davies is a freelance writer and investigative journalist, specialising in crime and poverty. He writes for *The Guardian* , has made documentaries for *World in Action* and has recently published *Dark Heart,* an investigation into the underclass in Britain.

Michele Elliott is a child psychologist and the Director and founder of the child protection charity *Kidscape.* She is the author of numerous books and articles and has chaired Home Office and World Health Organisation committees. She is a Winston Churchill Fellow and is the mother of two teenage sons.

Sophie Hughes has had twenty years experience as a practitioner and manager in children's services. Her current position includes responsibility for co-ordination of planning and review for looked-after children and the chairing of child protection conferences in Herefordshire.

Roger Kennedy has been consultant psychotherapist to the family unit at the Cassel Hospital for the last fifteen years. He is an honorary senior lecturer in psychiatry at the Charing Cross and Westminster and Chelsea Medical Schools and is a training analyst for the British Psychoanalytical Society. He has written several books and papers. His latest book is *Child Abuse, Psychotherapy and the Law,* which has just been published.

Allan Levy QC is a specialist in child law and medical law. He represented the Department of Health at the Cleveland Child Abuse Inquiry in 1987 and chaired the Staffordshire "Pindown" Inquiry into institutional abuse in 1990/91 (co-authoring the final report with Barbara Kahan). He has appeared as counsel in leading cases concerning child abuse, adoption, the Children Act 1989, child abduction and human rights and has both edited and contributed to books on child abuse.

Mike Lewis is Divisional Commander in the Brighton division of Sussex Police. He served at various stations in Sussex before taking up a post within the Organisation and Planning Branch at Sussex Police Headquarters. He was seconded to the Royal Hong Kong Police, then returned to Sussex where he subsequently worked in the Force Inspectorate, the Chief Constable's Staff Office and the Personnel Department. Mike Lewis has also undertaken a period of duty with HM Inspectorate of Constabulary.

Gill Mackenzie is Chief Probation Officer of the Gloucestershire Probation Service. She is Vice-Chair of the Association of Chief Officers of Probation (ACOP) and in that capacity is the lead officer on matters to do with risk management and work with sex offenders.

Terry Oates is a Detective Inspector in the Cheshire Constabulary, having completed 25 years service in the force, the vast majority of that time being within the criminal investigation departments. In 1994 he was the senior investigating officer in a major child abuse inquiry conducted within Cheshire. This inquiry was in many ways unique, in that it was historical and attempted to trace every former resident of the children's homes involved in the murder investigation. To date a total of 16 paedophiles have been convicted of offences committed during the 1960 - 80s.

George Smith is a Detective Chief Inspector with Sussex Police and has been in charge of the CID at Brighton since 1994. His work has involved his leading many murder investigations. He has been a career detective, having worked in the divisional CID at each rank. He has been in charge of the CID Training Department and was a member of the Fraud Squad for four years. A two year secondment took him to the USA, where he worked with the FBI.. Between October 1997 and February 1998 he was involved in dealing with a convicted paedophile, who arrived in Brighton and was the subject of intense media and police scrutiny which resulted in his being kept on a voluntary basis for four months at a local police station. He is currently a member of the ACPO working party set up to review the working practices of the National Criminal Intelligence Service Paedophile Unit.

John Staps is Head of Youth and the Vice Squad for Rotterdam Police, the Netherlands, and has held these posts for six years. His unit deals with all criminals up to the age of 18 and with sex offenders of all ages. John Staps has been in the Rotterdam Police Force for 17 years.

Sir William Utting held senior positions in the probation service, local and central government. He retired from the Department of Health in 1991 as Chief Inspector of Social services. He is now largely involved in voluntary work and is a member of the Committee on Standards of Conduct in Public Life. He has most recently chaired the *Review of the Safeguards for Children Living Away from Home,* the report of which was published in November, 1997

Ray Wyre is a nationally acknowledged expert in the sexual crime field. He began working with sex offenders while a member of the probation service in the 1970s. He then established a group work programme for sex offenders in a top security prison. Ray Wyre founded the Gracewell Clinic and Institute in Birmingham in 1988 and is now an independent sexual crime consultant and principal adviser to the Lucy Faithfull Foundation. As a Churchill Fellow he researched the treatment of both sex offenders and their victims in America. He appears in court as an independent expert witness, works closely with the police in many areas, has published numerous articles and has written several books.

ISTD PUBLICATIONS

- **The ISTD Handbook Of Community Programmes (2nd Edition)**
  Compiled and edited by Carol Martin. Information included in this edition comprises programmes across the UK (including Scotland and N. Ireland for the first time) for young people aged 10-25. The 300+ schemes and projects described are aimed not only at young and juvenile offenders but those who may be disadvantaged and excluded from school as well as those considered to be 'at risk'. Publication May 1998. c400 pages. ISBN 0 901541 53 2
- **A Guide To Setting Up And Evaluating Programmes For Young Offenders**
  By Simon Merrington. Foreword by James McGuire. This guide is the perfect companion to the ISTD Handbook of Community Programmes (2nd edition) and has been written as a source book for practical advice. Publication May 1998. 104 pages. ISBN 0 901541 55 9
- **The Forgotten Children: Young People In Prison**
  Selected and edited papers from three conferences held in 1997, at HMYOI Stoke Heath, HMYOI Portland and King's College London, which looked at the needs of imprisoned juveniles and young offenders. Edited by Stephanie Hayman with Carol Martin and Angus Nurse. 63 pages. Published April 1998. ISBN 0 901541 52 4
- **Imprisoning Women: Recognising Difference**
  Edited by Stephanie Hayman. Collected and edited papers from a conference held at HMP & YOI Styal in October 1997. Published March 1998. ISBN 0 901541 51 6
- **Deaths of Offenders The Hidden Side of Justice**
  Edited by Alison Liebling. Includes papers originally given at the third international conference on Deaths in Custody held at Brunel University, under the auspices of the ISTD. This third publication contains new material from the United Kingdom and other countries about deaths of offenders/detainees in the community as well as in police, prison or special hospital custody.260 pages. Published January 1998. ISBN 0 901541 48 6
- **The Directory of Criminology.** The first guide to UK institutions in which criminology is taught and researched, and the courses available, together with the individuals involved and their research interests. 195pp. Published 1995. Members: **£6.50** Non-members: **£11.50**

OCCASIONAL PAPERS:

- **Inspectorate Independence: Desirable or Essential?** AGM 1996 Address by Sir David Ramsbotham, HM Chief Inspector of Prisons. **£1.50**
- **Eve Saville Memorial Lecture 1995 - Between Prison and Probation: the Development of Intermediate Sanctions in Western Countries.** Professor Michael Tonry, University of Minnesota. **£1.50**
- **Eve Saville Memorial Lecture 1994: The Courts & the Challenges of the Multi-Cultural Society.** Mr Justice Brooke, Chairman of the Law Commission. **£1.50**
- **Eve Saville Memorial Lecture 1993: Handling Persistent Young Offenders: Next Steps.** John Harding, Chief Probation Officer, Inner London Probation Service. **£1.50**
- **Psychopathy: A legal and clinical dilemma.** Dr John Reed. AGM 94 Address. **£1.50**

- **Understanding the Paedophile.** (published jointly with the Portman Clinic) 32pp (1989) **£3.00**
- **History of the ISTD** - David Rumney and Eve Saville. Ed. Adrian Arnold. 144pp. (1992) **£5.00**

CONFERENCE REPORTS

- **Deaths in Custody: Caring for People at Risk.**
  Ed. Alison Liebling. Published by Whiting & Birch. *Contributions from*: Sir Louis Blom-Cooper, Ian Dunbar, Lindsey Hayes, Alison Liebling, David McDonald, Gethin Morgan, Rod Morgan, David Neal, Terry Waite and selected seminar papers from the ISTD conference organised in Cambridge in 1994. Published December 1996. 226 pp. *Special price from ISTD.* **£12.00**
- **Absent from School: Truancy & Exclusion.** Eds. Carol Martin and Stephanie Hayman. A combined report from ISTD's two conferences on this theme, held in February (London) and September (Manchester) 1996. *Contributions from:* Marva Buchanan, Avril Calder, Sue Chesterton, Angela Devlin, Lorna Farrington, Liz Jones, Edwin Lewis, Nicola Mackereth, Carl Parsons, John Simkins & Patrick Younge. Published February 1997. 66 pp. **£7.00**
- **Does Punishment Work?**
  Proceedings of a conference organised by **ISTD, The What Works Group** and **Positive Justice** in November 1995 and edited by James McGuire and Beverley Rowson. *Contributions from*: Derek E Blackman, Charmian Bollinger, David Carson, Danny Clark, Andrew Coyle, David Garland, Bryan Gibson, Malcolm Gillan, Patricia Green, Leroy Logan, Doris Layton MacKenzie, Sue McCormick, James McGuire, Jerome Miller, Philip Priestley, Jenny Roberts, Michael Schluter, Joanna Shapland, Stephen Shaw, Rosemary Thomson, Martin Wasik, Dick Whitfield, Rt Hon Ann Widdecombe MP, Jean Wynne. (1996) 88pp. **£7.00**
- **What Works with Young Prisoners?**
  Collected papers from a conference organised by ISTD with the Trust for the Study of Adolescence at HMYOI & RC Glen Parva in November 1995. Ed. Stephanie Hayman. **Plenary Presentations:** Susan Bailey, Roger Bullock, Roger Graef, Alison Liebling **Seminar contributions:** Linda Blud, Sue Evershed, Juliet Lyon, Jane Mardon, Martin McHugh, Mary McMurran, Glen Thomas, Barbara Tudor, David Waplington, Boyd Whitehead. 52pp. **£6.00**
- **Managing Risk: Achieving the Possible**
  Collected papers from a conference organised by ISTD in April 1995. Eds. Julia Braggins and Carol Martin. **Plenary presentations:** Sir Louis Blom-Cooper, David Carson, Glynn Harrison, Andrew von Hirsch, Richard Lingham, Judge Christopher Pitchers, Judith Pitchers, John Reed, Baden Skitt, Graham Smith, Richard Tilt, John Wadham, Jayne Zito. **Seminar contributions:** Walter Brennan, Tom Swan, Mitch Egan, Christine Lawrie, Ruth Mann, Barry Mitchell, Herschel Prins, Roger Tarling, Hilde Tubex, 90pp. **£7.00**
- **Dealing with Drugs: A new philosophy?**
  Collected papers from a conference organised by ISTD in March 1995.Ed. Carol Martin. Papers by Denis O'Connor, Nicholas Dorn & Toby Seddon, John Grieve, Mike Hindson, Howard Parker & Fiona Measham and Nigel South. 40pp. **£6.00**
- **Serious Young Offenders: Security, Treatment & Future Prospects.**
  A report of the conference organised by the ISTD in October 1994. Eds. Ian Heritage and Carol Martin. Papers by Malcolm Stevens, Dr Sue Bailey and Professor Eugene Ostapiuk. 32pp. **£6.00**

- **Contracts to Punish: Private or Public?** Collected papers from a conference organised by ISTD in Manchester in November 1994. Ed. Carol Martin. Papers by Paul Cavadino, Robin Halward, Ken Pease, Mick Ryan and Stephen Shaw. 32pp. **£6.00**
- **Resolving Crime in the Community: Mediation in Criminal Justice.** Collected papers from a conference organised by ISTD and the London Victim-Offender Mediation Network in September 1994. Papers from John Braithwaite, Australian National University; Teresea Reynolds, Victim Support; Terry O'Connell, New South Wales Police Service. Ed. Carol Martin. 32pp. **£6.00**
- **Victim Offender Mediation.** A report of the conference held jointly by ISTD and Mediation UK in London in February 1994. Papers by Marian Liebmann, Eric Morrell & Philip Priestley. 20pp. **£1.50**
- **Changing Policing: Business or Service?** A report of the Mannheim Centre/ISTD conference held in September 1993 at the London School of Economics. Ed. Carol Martin. 44pp. **£5.00**
- **Prison and After: What Works?** A report of ISTD's international residential conference held in Royal Holloway College in April 1993. Ed. Nic Groombridge. 56pp. **£6.00**
- **Values for Change: Mental Health Services in a Secure Environment.** A report of the MIND/ISTD conference held in November 1992 at King's College London. Ed. Ian Bynoe. 48pp. **£6.00**

CRIMINAL JUSTICE MATTERS provides information and informed opinion on all aspects of criminal justice including the police, the magistracy, crime prevention, forensic psychiatry, prisons, victims, women and crime, the law, probation and the judiciary both in Britain and abroad.

DESIGNED to be accessible and readable, CJM is essential reading for all who are concerned about crime and who want to be informed about the criminal justice process.

RECENT ARTICLES INCLUDE:

Howard Parker on the New Drug Users
Frances Heidensohn on Women in Policing
Betsy Stanko on Gender & Crime
David Garland on Surveillance and Society
Herschel Prins on Mental Disorders and Crime
Andrew Ashworth on Sentencing and Fairness
Russell Dobash et al on Steroids and Violence
Roy Porter on the History of the 'Drugs Problem'
An Interview with *James Q Wilson*
Michael Howard on the Crime Bill
Vivien Stern on prisons in Western Europe
John Muncie on 'The Youth Problem'
An Interview with *Frances Lawrence*
Leonard Leigh on the Criminal Cases Review
  Commission
Charles Pollard on restorative justice
Keith Hellawell on drugs strategy

BACK ISSUES AVAILABLE:

CJM No. 9 (Criminal Justice Act 1991) £2.00
CJM No. 11 (Crime & Media) £2.50
CJM No. 12 (Taking Drugs) £2.50
CJM No. 13 (Crime in Northern Ireland) £2.50
CJM No. 20 (Surveillance) £3.00
CJM No. 21 (Mental Disorder & Criminal Justice) £3.00
CJM No. 22 (Courting Justice) £3.00
CJM No. 23 (Sport and Crime) £3.00
CJM No. 24 (Debating Drugs) £3.00
CJM No. 25 (Crime & Justice USA) £3.00
CJM No. 26 (Law and Order Politics) £4.00
CJM No. 27 (Crime & Justice in Europe) £4.00
CJM No. 28 (Young People in Trouble) £4.00
CJM No. 29 (Justice Undermined) £4.00
CJM No. 30 (Prisons Today) £4.00
CJM No. 31 (Crime and Disorder) £4.00
CJM No. 32 (Policing) £4.00

Please write to ISTD for further information about all ISTD publications.

Published by the ISTD, King's College London, Strand, London WC2R 2LS
ISSN: 0962-7251